THE LIVING SHORE

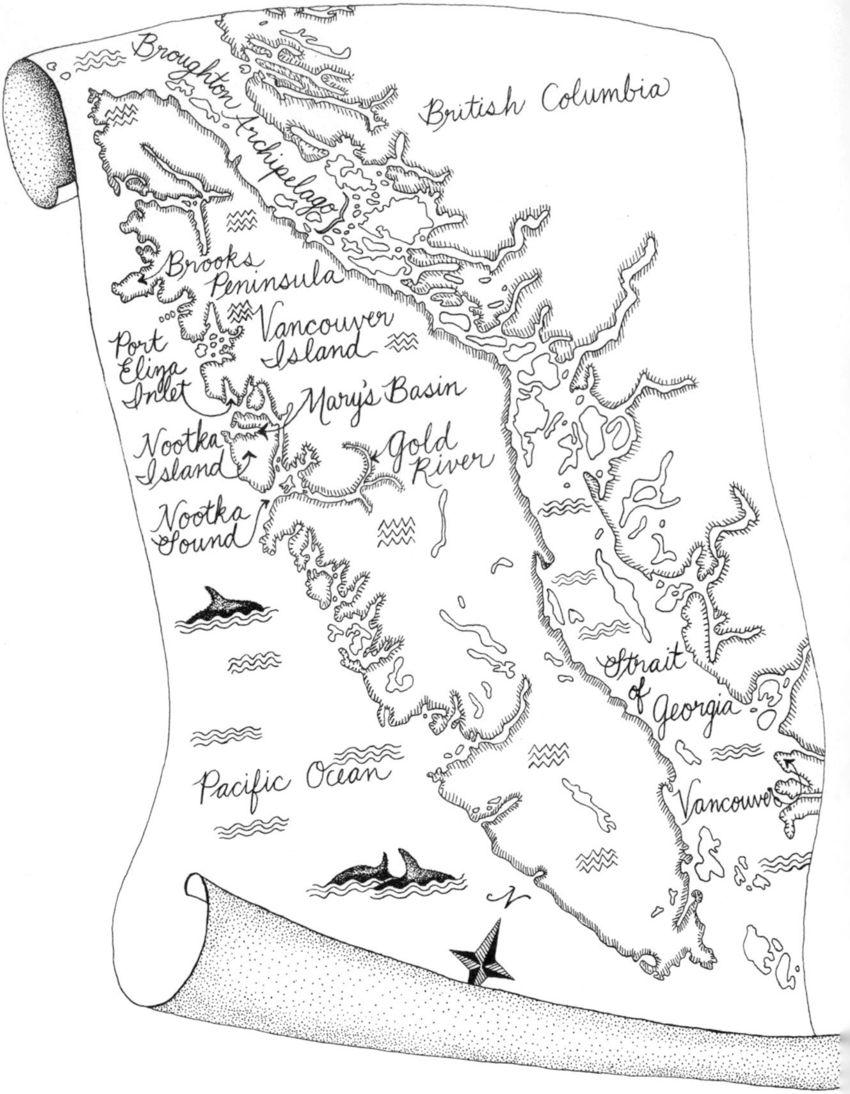
Broughton Archipelago
British Columbia
Brooks Peninsula
Vancouver Island
Port Eliza Inlet
Mary's Basin
Nootka Island
Gold River
Nootka Sound
Strait of Georgia
Pacific Ocean
Vancouver
N

THE LIVING SHORE

Rediscovering a Lost World

Rowan Jacobsen

Illustrations by Mary Elder Jacobsen

BLOOMSBURY

NEW YORK   BERLIN   LONDON

Published by Bloomsbury USA, New York

All papers used by Bloomsbury USA are natural, recyclable products made from wood grown in well-managed forests. The manufacturing processes conform to the environmental regulations of the country of origin.

LIBRARY OF CONGRESS CATALOGING–IN–PUBLICATION DATA

Jacobsen, Rowan.
The living shore : rediscovering a lost world /
Rowan Jacobsen.—1st U.S. ed.
p.   cm.
Includes bibliographical references and index.
ISBN-13: 978-1-59691-684-5 (hardcover)
ISBN-10: 1-59691-684-2 (hardcover)
1. Oyster culture—Washington (State)—Puget Sound.
2. Oyster fisheries—British Columbia—Vancouver Island.
3. Olympia oyster—Conservation.   4. Puget Sound Watershed
(Wash.)—Environmental conditions.   I. Title.
SH365.W2J33 2009
639.9'20916432—dc22
2009008903

First U.S. Edition 2009

1 3 5 7 9 10 8 6 4 2

Typeset by Westchester Book Group

Printed in the United States of America by Quebecor World Fairfield

CONTENTS

TIDES

*W*HEN THE FULL *moon hauls back the waters, they emerge, a glittering band along the shore, like doubloons washed up from the wreck of a Spanish galleon. They close their shells tight and, for a few hours, become land. Bears slip out of the cedary woods and trundle over them, picking at small fish that lingered too long. From a distance you might think they were glinting rocks, just another cobbly beach, rather than acres of living coastline. But if you stepped out of your boat and explored, old shells popping softly beneath your boots, you'd smell their salt-spray aroma and hear the crackling of receding water droplets and know*

that they were the living sea itself, holding on to the land to keep it from squirming away. And if you sat down among them and pried open some shells and tipped the briny flesh into your mouth, you might get some sense of how it had always been.

Then the moon lets go and the water returns, snaking along the low points, bubbling up like springs from under the shells. Soon they are covered, and they phase back to their other existence. They open their shells and drink in the sea. The bears withdraw and sixteen-armed purple sea stars pull their way up the tide's advancing edge, gobbling as they go. Tiny creatures hunker down beneath the shells, within the shells, spinning out little lives in a biogenic world. For a few hours, they disappear beneath the waves. And if you arrived at high water and didn't take the time to poke around, or if you were from some place where the land and the water have already come unglued and you assumed that the world you knew was the one that had always been, then you'd probably keep on going, and you'd never even know they existed at all.

FIRST CONTACT

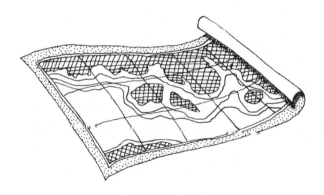

IN THE EARLY 1990s, a young Canadian marine biologist named Brian Kingzett scored an ecologist's dream job. The province of British Columbia wanted to know how much of its Swiss-cheese coastline had the potential for shellfish aquaculture. Most shellfish live in estuaries—bays or inlets sheltered from the open ocean—and BC was rich in such areas. Shellfish aquaculture is a form of intertidal farming. You obtain "seed"—baby shellfish resembling grains of sand—from a hatchery, plant it on beaches or mudflats, then harvest the shellfish when they mature in two to three years. Shellfish aquaculture has become a huge worldwide industry, as well as an important restoration tool—because shellfish feed by filtering algae out of water, they are an estuary's way of keeping itself clean and healthy. Eager to utilize its natural resources, whether logging, mining, or seafood, and with vast stretches of wild coastline under provincial control, BC embraced shellfish farming in the early nineties.

British Columbia has a staggering 16,780 miles of filigreed coastline, thanks to the glaciers that whittled fjords out of its ridges during the last ice age. Much of this coastline is on Vancouver Island, the largest island on the west coast of North America. A 450-mile-long outrider kissing the coast of Canada, Vancouver Island was not originally part of North America, nor even of Pangaea, the übercontinent formed by all seven of today's continents. Instead, the earth's mantle burped Vancouver Island into the South Pacific four hundred million years ago. The island began a jaunt across the Pacific, slamming into North America one hundred million years ago. But, like an immigrant holding on to her culture, it never quite assimilated with the rest of North America. By staying a few miles offshore, it provided the BC mainland with an epic breakwater sheltering a sailor's paradise of blue waters, snowy peaks, and protected inlets.

Vancouver Island was full of beaches and mudflats that might be suitable for both shellfish and the farmers who would be harvesting them, but many were hidden amid long stretches of fjord too steep for aquaculture. BC couldn't exactly convince shellfish farmers to head out into the wilderness if it couldn't tell them where to go. It needed the equivalent of a real estate catalog for shellfish farms. So in the early 1990s the Ministry of Agriculture, Fisheries, and Food put out a request for proposal on a contract to catalog the entire coast.

At the time, Brian Kingzett was a twentysomething consulting biologist for a firm called Aquametrix Research. He'd coauthored a paper titled "Biophysical Criteria for Shellfish Culture in British Columbia: A Site Capability Evaluation System." He'd also just started his own oyster farm. He needed to do something to support his "oyster habit," as he called it, which had yet to turn a profit, and the adventure of exploring BC appealed deeply to him. Aquametrix had calculated the bare minimum it would need to do the job, submitted its bid, and won. Kingzett became the latest in a long line of explorers, going back to James Cook and George Vancouver, commissioned to mess about in boats along the wildest coast in North America.

It was a dream job, but not an easy one. Water temperatures hung in the forties and fifties year-round. In winter the North Pacific catapulted storm after storm into the battlements of the coast, shutting down all boat traffic for days at a time. The only safe months were July and August, and even then the winds and swell were often too much for small boats like Kingzett's. To make the most of his seasonal window, he had to camp for weeks in the BC wilderness. That was just fine with him. He couldn't think of a better way to spend what would become his next seven summers.

Kingzett soon had his routine down. He'd travel a piece of coastline, cataloging every beach bigger than half an acre. From his boat he'd estimate the beach's size and slope and the distance between high and low water marks. Then he'd go ashore, note whether the sediment was mud, sand, or cobble, and snap a photo from the mid-tide line looking down the beach. He'd find an area of representative sediment and dig into it, looking for clams, the best indicators of what that beach could produce. He'd note if there were any predators such as sea stars (what used to be called starfish), which are voracious consumers of shellfish.

After recording all his data, Kingzett would write a line or two summarizing the beach. Often his notes would be brief: "Soft mud estuary." But anytime he saw something anomalous, he would write it down. All the information and photographs went into an online database keyed to a map of the BC coast.

In the course of his travels, Kingzett came to know the coast like few others. He startled flocks of sandhill cranes that scattered croaking into the sky. He saw natural luminescence in the water so strong that sea otters left glowing trails like shooting stars as they dove. He anchored near remote hot springs and convinced the local Tsimshian First Nations to show him hidden petroglyph carvings along the shoreline. He saw signs of ancient First Nation activity on many beaches and was always careful to note what he called "anthropogenic changes": rock fish traps built centuries ago by natives, and strange symmetrical lines in the sand, always right at the low-tide line, that he couldn't quite make sense of. He saw a lot of these in the Broughton Archipelago, a jumble of islands snuggled between Vancouver Island and the BC mainland. While in the Broughtons he also saw a mysterious helicopter flying a hundred meters over the coast, seemingly surveying the same areas he was.

By the summer of 1995 Kingzett had surveyed about four hundred of the two thousand beaches he'd eventually cover. He was working in the vicinity of Nootka Island, a remote stretch of coast even by BC standards. The green slopes of Nootka Island hit the water at a steep grade and plunged into the depths, leaving nowhere to get a purchase. However, wherever a stream flowed down from the island's peaks, ten thousand years of outwash had built up a cobbly shelf that formed a pocket beach. No sane shellfish farmer would choose such a spot, but Kingzett needed to survey them anyway.

The cobble on such beaches dropped straight into the abyss, which allowed him to adopt a run-and-gun approach to cataloging them. He'd do a clockwise loop of the fjord, stopping at every beach. He'd nose the boat right into the beach, leave the motor down and idling, throw an anchor over the bow, and literally run off the front of the boat with his rake, clipboard, and camera. Click, click, click, he'd get his data and photos, then push off and jump back on the boat. It was a bit sketchy, and with a promising site he'd have taken more time, but he figured he needed to do at least twelve beaches during every four-hour low tide just to stay on schedule. And by now, he was pretty sure he knew what he'd find at these spots. After you've surveyed your first hundred beaches, they start to fall into groups. After your first four hundred, you can almost drive by at thirty knots and fill out your data sheet.

One day Kingzett was hustling to make up for lost time. The day before he'd busted his propeller in a long inlet called Mary's Basin that has a notorious bottleneck. If you don't time the tides just right, you run aground. While fixing the prop, he'd heard a plop; the bushing—the metal cylinder on which the prop sits—had fallen into the water. He'd managed to rig a new bushing using a piece of copper pipe, but it was dodgy at best. More important, he'd lost half a day to the repair. He wanted to get the beaches surveyed and get the hell out of there. Kingzett had a partner boat running up the center of the fjords taking mid-channel salinity and temperature readings. If worst came to worst, he could have towed his boat home, but it would have been a long, long ride.

Kingzett motored into Port Eliza Inlet, nosed his boat onto the first beach, and leaped ashore, ready to jot down his notes. Then he stopped and stared. The beach looked like it was covered in old coins. They were huge drifts of *Ostrea conchaphila*, the Olympia oyster, the only native oyster of the Pacific coast of Canada and the United States. He knew they had been the basis of a fishery in British Columbia in the early twentieth century. Now you rarely saw them. That was enough to make him take notice. But that was all he knew about *Ostrea conchaphila*. No one in Canada specialized in the oyster anymore. He noted its presence, snapped some photos, then pushed on to the next beach. He filed a mental note deep in the back of his mind. Had he been near the end of his seven-year survey, he might have done more than that. But he was just beginning, and he had no way of knowing that only a handful of the two thousand beaches he would ultimately visit would be like this one. He had no way of knowing that here, in the middle of nowhere, in a dead-end inlet nobody ever visited, he was looking at one of the rarest beds of oysters in the world.

WHITE GOLD

WHEN GEORGE VANCOUVER explored the coastal clefts of the Pacific Northwest in his ship, *Discovery*, in 1792, he found them "plentifully strewn" with oysters. This was not exactly news to the hundreds of thousands of natives living in the area, who had been dining heartily on shellfish for millennia. Many of these tribes were famous for their salmon culture, but the less glamorous protein, the ham sandwich of 1000 B.C., lay right at their feet. Clams and oysters kept them alive. (They were the source of some good myths, too. One relates that clams were banished under the sand for being such gossips, and every low tide they clear their throats and continue to spout more

tittle-tattle.) Native villages often formed at the site of boun-
tiful oyster beds.

The oyster making those beds was the Olympia. It once
carpeted bays from California all the way up through British Columbia, and even showed up as far north as Sitka,
Alaska, and as far south as Panama, but nowhere else on
earth. Today only vestigial populations remain along most
of its historic range.

In addition to eating them raw, natives of hundreds or
thousands of years ago steamed, dried, and smoked shellfish. Whole villages would gather to process the harvest,
piling the shells high. Up and down the west coast, standing as monuments to that former abundance, are shell
middens—prehistoric compost piles.

Over the years, some of these shell mounds achieved
epic proportions. When people hear about middens, they
picture mounds the size of a truck, or maybe a house. But
the Emeryville Shellmound, south of Berkeley, California,
was 60 feet high and 350 feet in diameter—the size of a
high school stadium. Residents of the Pacific Northwest
still occasionally discover, when some ancient tree uproots
in a storm, that they have been living on a shell midden all
their lives. Some middens have been dated to four thousand years ago. Some are likely even older.

These middens make it clear that the shellfish beds were
incredibly productive—it takes a lot of people, a lot of
shellfish, and a lot of time to make piles that big—but not
quite productive enough. As a rule, middens have their

largest shells on the bottom. The most recent additions, at the top, are smaller. Olympia oysters, in particular, turn up in great abundance in the bottom layers, then suddenly disappear. Natives may have been better than Europeans at managing their resources, but they still followed the usual trend of eating their way through a shellfish community faster than the community could replenish itself. But for thousands of years, human populations on the coast were small enough to simply move on to the next, unexploited beds, allowing the exhausted beds to recover. The people kept eating, and the oysters held their own.

Then, on January 24, 1848, on the banks of the American River in California's Sierra Nevada, an event took place that forever changed the Olympia's fortunes. James Marshall, a foreman building a water-powered lumber mill for the agricultural pioneer John Sutter, noticed some shiny bits of metal in the water flowing out of the mill. Marshall and Sutter thought they knew what it was, and they tried to keep the discovery quiet. They failed. Soon Samuel Brannan, San Francisco's newspaper baron, who also just happened to have recently bought all the prospecting-supply stores in town, was parading through the streets with a vial of gold, shouting, "Gold! Gold! Gold from the American River!"

At the time, San Francisco was a two-bit port of perhaps a thousand people, and California was still part of Mexico, though under U.S. military control since the Mexican-American War. But by the end of the following year, more than a hundred thousand forty-niners had descended on

San Francisco and the hills beyond, and the city population swelled to nearly thirty thousand. A few of the lucky ones found gold. And a few of the clever ones realized that the easy money was not hiding in the hills but quietly opening and closing its shells all around San Francisco Bay.

For forty-niners who struck it rich, epic celebrations were obligatory. San Francisco had plenty of booze to fuel these celebrations, but very few foods worthy of marking such an event. It was not a fancy town. It was barely a town at all. Fortunately, its immense bay possessed billions of oysters, the perfect celebration food. New Yorkers always celebrated with oysters. Parisians always celebrated with oysters. And if it was good enough for them . . . *Oysters and champagne for all my friends, and their friends, too! In fact, oysters and champagne all around!*

Oysters sometimes went for a dollar apiece in 1850 San Francisco. There was probably more value in the bay's bivalves than in the hills' ore. A few enterprising locals made a killing gathering the wild oysters. Perhaps there were even real killings—San Francisco was virtually lawless at the time. Oystermen staked their claims to sections of tide flats in the Sausalito area and quickly fenced them off to discourage poachers. But the fences could do nothing about the silt already pouring out of the Sierra Nevada from hydraulic mining operations, which used high-pressure hoses to liquidate hillsides, and the oyster farmers were forced to move their yards to the less disturbed south bay. That bought them only a little time, because Olympias are

Oyster bed fence, San Francisco Bay, 1889. Photograph Gulf of Maine Cod Project, NOAA National Marine Sanctuaries; Courtesy of National Archives.

slow-growing oysters, taking five years to reach what is euphemistically referred to as market size, which, in the case of Olympias, still means it takes two thousand to make a gallon of meats (compared with two hundred for other species). A determined miner could down five hundred in a sitting. Demand far outpaced supply, and within a few short years San Francisco Bay was stripped clean of its living skin of oysters.

San Francisco continued to boom and to eat. The city cast its hungry gaze northward, and the oyster community vaporized as if a ray gun were strafing the coast. First went

Culling oysters in San Francisco Bay, 1889. Photograph Gulf of Maine Cod Project, NOAA National Marine Sanctuaries; Courtesy of National Archives.

Humboldt Bay, then Oregon's Yaquina Bay. In 1851 San Francisco found Shoalwater Bay (today known as Willapa Bay), a huge, shallow estuary in Washington State that is a virtual oyster factory. Twenty-five miles long, protected from ocean storms by a thin barrier beach, and unusually flat for a west coast bay, so that half its area is uncovered every low tide, Shoalwater was caked with Olympias. For that very reason, it had once been thick with Chinook Indians, too, but by the 1850s, after a few rounds of smallpox, only about a hundred natives remained. Soon they were employed by a handful of white settlers in the endeavor to harvest every last oyster in Shoalwater Bay. A veritable conveyer belt of boats carried the bounty to San Francisco.

Shoalwater was such rich ground that it withstood the onslaught for a surprisingly long time. In the 1890s it was still shipping more than one hundred thousand gallons of Olympias to San Francisco each year. But Olympia larvae need other Olympia shells to attach to (or "set" on), so once all those oysters had been shipped in their shells to San Francisco, revealing the naked mud of the bay, one of the great oyster estuaries on the planet stopped making new ones. By 1910 it was exhausted.

That put a halt to San Francisco's attempt to digest an entire species. No Olympias were left within traveling distance of the Bay City. Puget Sound sheltered more Olympias than any other place on earth. The Squaxin and neighboring tribes had been carefully tending oyster beds for millennia (and complaining, as early as the 1860s, that sediment from the settlers' upstream timber mills was burying their oyster beds), and it wasn't long before whites got in on the action. But attempts to transport those Olympias to California, in the days of slow sail and no refrigeration, ended with deckloads of putrid shellfish being unceremoniously dumped overboard.

Fortunately for the San Francisco oystermen, the transcontinental railroad had been completed in 1869 and was soon bringing carfuls of eastern oysters, which can survive out of water much longer than Olympias, to the west coast. The October 22, 1869, edition of the *Alta California*

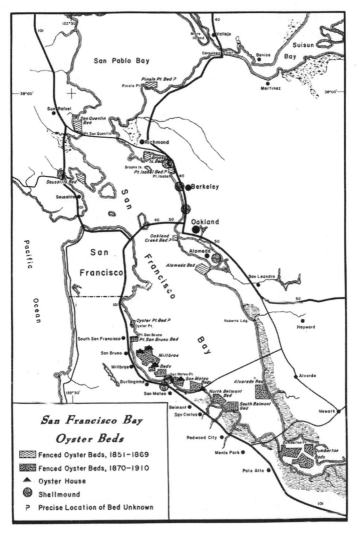

A map of the San Francisco Bay oyster beds. Courtesy California Department of Fish and Game.

excitedly announced the arrival: "The first carload of Baltimore and New York oysters in shells, cans, kegs, all in splendid order, has arrived, packed and shipped by the pioneer oyster house of the west, A. Booth, Chicago, Ill."

Oystermen were able to plant tens of thousands of bushels of baby eastern oysters in San Francisco Bay and carry on with a new and preferable species—a two-year-old eastern oyster is ten times the size of a four-year-old Olympia. Eastern oysters wouldn't reproduce in such cold water, so the business relied on fresh infusions of seed oysters from Chesapeake Bay every year, but they grew well, and the business became much more profitable than it ever had been with Olympias. Even before Shoalwater Bay ran out of its native oysters, 90 percent of the San Francisco market was being supplied by its eastern oyster beds. In his book *Tales of the Fish Patrol*, Jack London tells of being hired by an oyster farmer to insinuate himself into a group of oyster pirates who were robbing the beds at night. "We hauled the noses of the boats up on the shore side of a big shoal, and all hands, with sacks, spread out and began picking. Every now and again the clouds thinned before the face of the moon, and we could see the big oysters quite distinctly. In almost no time sacks were filled and carried back to the boats, where fresh ones were obtained." London captured those pirates, but it was not enough to save the San Francisco oyster industry, which was done in by pollution.

And what about the billions of Olympias stuck in Puget Sound? Well, they may not have been able to reach the market, but eventually the market came to them. Around 1900, Puget Sound, the largest and most resilient of west coast estuaries, surpassed Shoalwater Bay in Olympia production, supplying Seattle and other frontier towns. The northern half of Puget Sound is deep and steep, not good shellfish habitat, but the southern end, near the town of Olympia, is a tangle of finger inlets featuring long mudflats fed by freshwater creeks that nurture thick algae populations—a smorgasbord for bivalves. By 1910, they held the only commercially viable populations of Olympias in the world.

And that, of course, is why we call them "Olympias." It's a provincial name for an oyster that used to blanket the coast of multiple countries, and it underscores the decimation of the species. In British Columbia they are simply called "native oysters." But the eastern oyster of Canada and the United States is every bit as native. Taking a cue from Canada's First Nations people, I'm tempted to call them First Oysters (the ones before the invasives arrived), but most people who work with the oysters refer to them by their shortened name, Oly (rhymes with "holy"), and so will I.

Blessed with a little more time than their Shoalwater counterparts, the oyster farmers of the South Sound managed some breakthroughs in oyster culture that bought them a few decades. They realized the importance of having shell for the new oyster larvae to attach to and began adding layers of fresh shell, known as "cultch," to their beds right before spawning season. In essence, they made the switch from hunter-gatherer to farmer. They also noticed that Olys died if exposed to particularly hot or cold temperatures, such as might occur during low tides at midsummer or midwinter. So they began the process of diking: adding log or concrete berms that would trap the receding tide and keep the oysters covered, regulating their temperature.

These last healthy Oly populations held on in their nooks and crannies until the dread year of 1927, when a pulp mill in Washington's Oakland Bay began flooding the inlet with sulfites, finishing off the oysters and everything that went with them. The west coast oyster industry reinvented itself with the Pacific oyster, a weedlike Japanese export that did surprisingly well in the sulfite-laden sound.

In British Columbia, on the sheltered side of Vancouver Island, a significant Oly population held on in Ladysmith Harbour until 1929, when a freak cold snap killed them. With that, the oyster industry in BC, which had never been large, expired.

In 1957 the Oakland Bay pulp mill closed its doors for good. Slowly, the water quality of Puget Sound improved, and oyster farmers might once again have raised Olys. But in the thirty years that had elapsed, the farmers had fallen for the Pacific oyster. It grew huge in a year, didn't care about cold or heat, was more tolerant of pollution, could last far longer out of the water during transport, and had a more general diet than the Oly. Like rats and cockroaches and human beings, it was well adapted to the new world order. It has now taken over most of the world supply, from Europe to Australia to the United States. In a nod to their roots, a few of the century-old oyster companies in South Sound, including the Olympia Oyster Company, Little Skookum Shellfish Growers, and Taylor Shellfish Farms, continue to farm small plots of Olys; everyone else has abandoned the Oly to the wilds.

There, the little oyster has done better than expected. It hasn't established many new beachheads, but it hasn't died out, either. It still lurks in most of its old haunts, though usually just a few individuals are found here and there. These refugees serve as a reminder of what once was as irreplaceable an ecosystem as the California redwoods. Today, a single bay in Puget Sound holds the last healthy ecosystem of Olys—or so everyone thought.

GHOST CREATURES

In July 2008, at a boat launch not far from the coma-
tose timber town of Gold River, I stepped onto the MV
Atrevida, a research vessel on loan from Vancouver Island
University, and slid into the Nootka fjords. Ten thousand
years ago, when the glaciers stopped flaying this island, its
west coast had become a network of gouged river valleys.
Then the earth warmed, sea levels rose steadily for five
millennia, and long tongues of ocean licked inland as far
as fifty miles. For a while, Gold River boomed on one of
those deep intrusions, but a few years ago the timber industry tanked and the pulp mill dematerialized, carted off

piece by piece. Gold River is attempting to reinvent itself as a sportfishing mecca despite spotty salmon runs in recent years.

The *Atrevida* pulled away from the boat launch, banked around a spur of hemlocks, and burrowed west down Muchalat Inlet, following a blue ribbon through a steep evergreen V. The fjord was too narrow, and the slopes too steep, to see anything beyond our immediate surroundings, though occasionally, where one inlet met another, glimpses opened up of the four-thousand-foot peaks looming over us. As Slartibartfast, the planet designer in *The Hitchhiker's Guide to the Galaxy*, says, fjords give a lovely baroque feel to a continent.

I was part of a nine-member expedition, parceled out among the *Atrevida* and an accompanying rigid-hulled inflatable, that would spend the next week on the lonely rim of the fjords, looking for oysters. We hoped to find Brian Kingzett's Oly beds, if they still existed, and learn *why* they still existed.

Betsy Peabody, executive director of the Puget Sound Restoration Fund (PSRF), had spent two years organizing the trip. The PSRF, founded by Peabody in 1997, is devoted to restoring Olys and other key species to Puget Sound. Its motive is simple: to make Puget Sound the spectacular home that it used to be. "We live in this place," Betsy had said as we spent a day traversing the Northwest by car and ferry from Puget Sound to Gold River. "Wouldn't we love to experience that sense of plenty? That sense of resources that are there to enjoy. Wouldn't it be nice to try to re-create that? It's not an impossible goal."

What I love about Betsy and her organization are the can-do attitude and the emphasis on reestablishing the productive coexistence of people and natural systems, rather than enforcing a separation. It's part of a sea change under way in the conservation world—a realization that we long not just to save wild places but also to be reintegrated with them. "I'm not looking to lock stuff up," she told me. "I'm looking toward our enjoyment of this place. Bringing it back so that we can be a part of it. Which we always were."

Olys were always an important part of the scene in Puget Sound, feeding humans and other animals, keeping the water clean, and providing shelter for numerous tiny creatures. But in Puget Sound most remaining Oly populations are tiny and semi-functional, often dependent on human structures, such as dikes, for their tenuous existence. Learning about the species and its ways from these remnant populations is like learning about traditional Native American society by studying a modern reservation. Hence Betsy's excitement when she first met Brian Kingzett at a shellfish conference in 2006. He asked her what she did. She told him about her Oly restoration efforts. He said, that's funny, eleven years ago he'd come across acres of those little guys. From that moment, Betsy began plotting this trip.

Betsy is small and lean, with Sandy Duncan hair. She might weigh a hundred pounds dripping wet in hip waders, which she often is, yet she easily commands a group, channeling consensus into action. That skill has served her well at the PSRF, which she formed after burning out on traditional government and nonprofit work. "I did not want to do any advocacy work," she told me. "I didn't want to work on policies. There are very well-established organizations that do that. I wanted to do work that I find interesting, that I feel is really worth doing, and that is *always* results-oriented and project-oriented. I don't want to be talking to people who are actually doing it. I want to be experiencing it myself. I feel like it's been a journey of authentication for me, after working on these issues two steps removed."

The PSRF isn't one of the larger groups restoring oyster populations. In fact, it's quite small. Yet, like its diminutive subject and executive director, the organization's exuberant character has had an outsize influence on its world.

"We started out very small, with zero resources," Betsy said. "We had nothing. But we felt that we could add value by directing resources toward projects that needed to get done. Stuff that would enrich the lives of people who live in this area, that would help to restore the assemblage of creatures known to exist in this place historically."

Oysters soon became a natural focus. "Most projects in Puget Sound are salmon-related. Salmon is the iconic species. It's the basis for a lot of funding that comes from the federal government. When you have salmon species that are the basis of commercial fisheries and are on the Endangered Species List, they get the whole engine going. So we gravitated toward species that were not receiving that kind of attention. No one was doing anything with shellfish. The state actually developed a rebuilding plan for Olympia oysters, but it wasn't funded. Weirdly, the fact that it wasn't funded allowed the project to be undertaken by a lot of sectors of the community. We had some built-in expertise because Bill Taylor [of Taylor Shellfish Farms] was on our board, and his family had been cultivating Olympias for four generations. We figured we could work under his wing and learn how to produce seed and identify suitable habitat. We decided to take that on. It's been a really interesting journey, but there's a lot more to do, and so we're going north to Vancouver Island to learn what we can."

A diverse crew was joining Betsy on the search for these BC oysters. Mike Beck, senior scientist for the Nature Conservancy's Global Marine Initiative, wanted to study some of the last functional pieces of an ecosystem that had once been a major factor in the life of the western coast. Sarah Davies of Canada's Department of Fisheries and Oceans was along to take the pulse of this Canadian species of special concern. Joth Davis, lead researcher for Taylor Shellfish Farms, and Brian Allen, staff ecologist for the PSRF, had been studying what Olys need to thrive and what we can do to help them. They were as excited about the trip as anthropologists pursuing rumors of a tribe in New Guinea still unaffected by civilization. David Hyde, a producer at KUOW-FM, Seattle's National Public Radio affiliate, saw the journey in much the same way and thought it would make an excellent radio adventure.

Brian Kingzett was guiding the expedition. Kingzett had become the point person in the creation of Vancouver Island University's Deep Bay Field Station, which will co-ordinate the efforts of British Columbia's marine ecologists, aquaculture industry, and culinary industry to create a sustainable enterprise, but on this particular journey his role was that of guide. He was, after all, the only person who knew where we were going. He piloted the inflatable while Stephanie Richards, a blonde, fiftyish woman with a fifty-ton skipper's ticket, captained the *Atrevida*. In a past life, Richards had operated a sixty-foot ex–seine boat servicing fish farms and crew boats for loggers in open waters, and she was the only one on the trip who could confidently wear dangly earrings and pink mudboots at the helm of a research vessel.

And I made nine. A few years ago I wrote a book called *A Geography of Oysters*. I'd long been fascinated by the hundreds of varieties of oysters available in North America, each with a distinct appearance and flavor. For my book I explored the geography of America's coasts and tried to discern what makes a great oyster. During my travels I fell in love with one tiny oyster in particular. The Oly's coppery, smoked-mushroom sweetness is unlike anything else in the world. It has something original to say. Tasting Olys amid the usual mix of eastern and Pacific oysters was like having a foreign dignitary at a dinner party of my friends. The new perspective enlightened, entertained, and even made the familiar voices more re-freshing. I loved checking in with the Oly from time to time, being reminded that in a few inlets in southern Puget Sound, life was manifesting itself in a unique way. But I also worried that a few shifts in the market or land-scape could make it virtually impossible to interact with this oyster again. I had met Betsy while researching Olys for my book. When she mentioned this trip, I talked my way aboard.

The unlikely guiding spirit for our journey was John Steinbeck, who in 1940, flush from the success of *The Grapes of Wrath*, decided to collect invertebrates along the Pacific coast with his pal Ed Ricketts, publishing their findings as *The Log from the Sea of Cortez*. Steinbeck sailed out of Monterey on a trawler, turned south, and headed around the Baja Peninsula into the Gulf of California, while we went north to Canada, but in many ways his jour-ney paralleled our own. Like us, he was curious how ani-mals had survived in these coastal areas for thousands of years, intrigued by the exchange that transpires between the life and the place. He understood that the littoral com-munity hiding amid the rocks and tide pools was special, and he also realized that convincing Americans of its im-portance was a hard sell. He heard the drums of war along the coast as his country geared up for World War II, and he questioned whether he could justify squandering atten-tion on such insignificant creatures during a time of global turbulence:

If we seem a small factor in a huge pattern, nevertheless it is of relative importance. We take a tiny colony of soft corals from a rock in a little water world. And that isn't terribly important to the tide pool. Fifty miles away the Japanese shrimp boats are dredging with overlapping scoops, bringing up tons of shrimps, rapidly destroying the species so it may never come back, and with the species destroying the ecological balance of the whole region. That isn't very important in the world. And thousands of miles away the great bombs are falling and the stars are not moved thereby. None of it is important or all of it is.

By putting our lives on hold for a week and trekking to the edge of the continent to seek the smallest oyster in the world, we nine were firmly throwing ourselves in with the "all of it is important" camp.

Nootka Island snuggles into the curved embrace of Vancouver Island just as Vancouver Island does into the BC mainland. It's like a fractal, the pattern repeated on multiple scales. Our destination was a fractal one scale down, the Nuchatlitz Islands, a jumble of islets plugged into Nootka's Pacific side. There, on a lagoon sheltered from the swell, a good four hours from Gold River by fast boat, an oyster farmer named Bob Devault has made his home for thirty-four years. Bob, one of just a handful of residents on two-hundred-square-mile Nootka Island, lives perhaps twenty minutes from the site of Brian's Oly beds.

Bob has cisterns for water and turbines and solar panels for electricity, not to mention a few hundred thousand Pacific oysters hanging in the lagoon on ropes. Bob's place beats the hell out of camping.

But first we had to get there. We boated for hours through the canyonlike fjords, the evening shadows clocking from the western flanks to the water and finally rising up the eastern flanks. The windchill in the open boats went from bearable to brutal. In July, Vancouver Island stays light until ten at night, and you can make out shadows against the water until maybe eleven. Kingzett, who had picked his way through the rocky Nuchatlitz Islands exactly once before and had been urging us to keep moving all day long, grew increasingly tense as it became apparent that we might lose our race against the sun.

We passed hardly a boat. Eagles commanded the treetops near shore and black bears played in grassy patches along the water's edge. A face like a wizened and mustachioed kung fu expert slid past the boat. A sea otter. I begged Stephanie for a better look and she whipped the *Atrevida* around, but the otter dove. The otters of Nootka have learned that a boat with its engines at full throttle is all business and can be ignored. But a boat that stops, or worse, a nosy kayak—well, that ain't natural. They wink out like prairie dogs.

Kingzett, in the inflatable, caught up with us. "What's wrong?" he asked. "Why are you stopping?" I explained about the sea otter. He was silent for a moment, then took a deep breath. "Okay," he said quietly, "no more stopping

A sea otter.

for otters." He opened up the throttle on the inflatable and sped off. We followed.

Kingzett has a complicated relationship with the otters. He doesn't deny that they have more charisma than Paul Newman. He knows that they are a key component of the ecosystem and that their recovery from the edge of extinction over the past twenty years is one of the most heartening stories in conservation. But he also knows that they are shellfish-consuming machines—urchins, mussels, abalone, clams, you name it. Unbelievably cute at a distance, they are, up close, five-foot-long, ninety-pound weasels that can eat twenty pounds of shellfish a day. They know just where the soft spot is in a bivalve's shell and just how to tap it out with a rock. They even excavate geoducks—gigantic clams that dig three feet down—leaving bomb craters in the sand. Our entire trip was riding on Kingzett being able to find his oyster beds again, and he worried that the otters might have cleaned them out. It had been fourteen otter-intensive years, after all, since he'd been there. "If we get out there and all we see is empty shell," he joked, "you may see me hanging my halibut gaff over the side of the boat, hunting otters!"

Otters have always been a driving force in the history of Nootka. When Captain James Cook arrived at Nootka Sound on March 29, 1778, becoming the first European to set foot on the west coast of what is now Canada, he encountered a thriving tribe of several thousand natives. The locals shouted "Nootka" at Cook when he arrived, and he took this to be their name for themselves and their island. What they were actually saying to him was "go around"— it's an island, buddy—but Cook and the rest of the world referred to them and their homeland as Nootka ever after. They called themselves the Nuu-chah-nulth, "people of the deer," a word that lives on in the name of the Nuchatlitz Islands.

The Nuu-chah-nulth proved to be eager traders, especially one chief named Maquinna, who astutely saw that becoming the intermediary between the locals and the Europeans was the key to power. Along a coast where they never knew when they might be attacked, the white traders welcomed Maquinna's hospitality, and soon Friendly Cove, his village on Nootka Sound, became the most important seaport north of Mexico.

It was all about the otters. Sea otter fur is the densest in the world, with more than one thousand hairs per square millimeter—a necessity to survive in the frigid North Pacific when you have no blubber. The traders arrived from Europe with metal goods and swapped them for otter pelts.

Then they sold the pelts in China, bought tea, and returned to Europe. Maquinna and his subjects showed no qualms about the wholesale harvest of the otters, who competed with them for shellfish and salmon. In fact, the archaeological record shows that the natives were already decimating the sea otter populations, and altering the coastal ecosystem in the process, 2,500 years ago.

Otter hunting must have become a lucrative full-time endeavor for some of the natives. The number of pelts in the records is staggering, considering how small some of these ships were. James Hanna, on the brig *Sea Otter*, sold 560 otter pelts in China for $20,000 in 1785. A year later, 2,552 otter pelts sold in China for $54,847. In 1787, 800 furs netted $30,000 in China. The great wealth to be made in the otter trade hastened the European rush to the coast. With the cooperation of the locals, tens of thousands of otter skins must have been delivered to China. But even this didn't finish off the otters; that took the improved technology and firepower of the industrial age, which enabled fur traders to eliminate sea otters from British Columbia in the 1920s. By then, the world population of sea otters was down from an estimated three hundred thousand to just a thousand.

Without the otters' steadying presence, the area transformed. A plague of sea urchins, the otters' favorite food, grazed its way through the kelp forests that lined the coasts—mirroring the clear-cuts perpetrated by human loggers on the slopes of Vancouver Island. Along with the kelp forests went all the species that lived in them. The few natives still living on the coasts didn't mind; the abundant sea urchins became a local delicacy, and generational memory is short. It's easy to forget about creatures you've heard about only from your grandparents.

Only in Alaska were some otters able to elude the fur trade. In the 1960s, eighty-nine Alaskan otters were reintroduced to the coast of Vancouver Island. Returned to prime otter habitat, with a stupendous smorgasbord of urchins laid out before them, they thrived. The area now holds the largest concentration of sea otters in the world, more than twenty-five hundred at last count. Sea urchins have declined, and the kelp forests—and many creatures that go with them—have returned.

While ecologists are thrilled by this turn of events, the sentiment is not unanimous. "I remember when a fishing boat came, everyone would gather at the docks to feast on sea urchins, clams, abalone and mussels," Leo Jacks, a First Nations elder, told *Canadian Geographic* magazine in 2006. "Our kids have never tasted sea urchins."

But the real worry is that their kids' kids may never taste wild salmon. Every few miles along Muchalat Inlet, the wilderness was broken by the mesh fencing and green metal square tower of what looked like a small prison rising out of the water—salmon farms.

The BC government has got the salmon farming religion. More than one hundred salmon farms line the coast of British Columbia. They hold twenty million Atlantic salmon, an entirely different genus from the native Pacifics. The arrival of all these salmon farms has coincided with the decline of wild salmon in BC. Activists believe this is because salmon farms spread pollution and sea lice—parasites that proliferate in the unnatural population densities of the pens. The industry cites research showing a negligible effect of farms on wild salmon. Whatever the truth, everyone agrees that wild BC salmon are imperiled.

While shellfish are the creatures that supported the shoreline ecosystem, salmon do the same for the upstream ecosystems. Born in clear, gravelly streams, salmon migrate to the sea during their youth, then, after a few years of exponential growth, return to their home rivers, swimming upstream all the way to their birthplace, where they spawn and die. They are, essentially, millions of pounds of high-quality marine protein and fertilizer delivering itself into the mountain rivers, and then, with the help of bears, otters, eagles, and others, spreading out to nourish the forest. A third of the nitrogen in BC valley floors was once salmon, as is 90 percent of the nitrogen in a grizzly bear.

Yet only a fraction of salmon still make these spawning runs. Dams and stream destruction are more to blame than fish farms. Reverberations from this collapse are still being felt throughout the Pacific Northwest. In his hypnotic book *Totem Salmon*, Freeman House writes, "Each creature, each organism, has some functional role in the web of life out of which it has emerged. The local field of being that we call the ecosystem must experience a period of adjustment when one of its organisms has disappeared—even if the disappearance has occurred over a period of time beyond human understanding. When people, accidentally or purposefully, experience engagement with these fields of being, the direct, ineffable sense of the ghosts of lost creatures may come visiting."

House compares this sense to a phantom limb. The brain subconsciously remembers what used to be. You wander the seashore, scanning the waves and picking up shells. You feel the exhilaration of the high-energy environment, two systems crashing together, but also feel strangely wistful. Some ancient part of you is thinking, *This used to mean much more.*

Freeman House senses the ghost salmon in his California river because he lived alongside it for years and learned its language. Eventually he became so intimate with the river that he could pick out the ghost whispers from the rest of the natural chatter: "Ecosystem absences can become a palpable presence, a weird stillness moving against the winds of existence and leaving a waveform of perturbation behind. . . . On a dark night by a river, the noise of which is a form of silence, such a ghost may find a voice in the human imagination."

But most of us never spend that dark night by a river. Estranged from any functioning ecosystem, we never learn the natural languages. Even if we hear the voices in our imagination, we can't make meaning of the babble.

It's the shifting-baseline phenomenon. We believe that what we experienced when we were kids is how it has always been. Apart from a few reminiscences from our elders, or the insistence of old books, we have no way of knowing that we are growing up in a diminished world. It's as if, when we were born, we inherited a quilt with a fraying edge that has been unraveling ever since. It's too fragile to use, though we still cherish it. We never saw the quilt in good condition, with edging intact, and believe that unraveling is simply what quilts do. By the time we pass the threadbare gift to our children, they won't believe us when we tell them it actually used to keep people warm.

As we pressed on into graying light and softening forms, the white V of our wake glowing behind us, I wondered if these fjords were unraveling. Could their integrity survive the clear-cuts and declining salmon? They certainly *felt* intact; there was a grandeur that you just don't find back east. In 1853, when oysters were already being extirpated from many of their traditional haunts on the east coast, Theodore Winthrop could still write in *The Canoe and the Saddle*, "Civilized mankind has never yet had a fresh chance of developing itself under grand and stirring influences so large as in the Northwest."

For the most part, the fresh chance is long gone. We remade most of the Northwest using the same model we employed elsewhere. We tamed it in ways we are no longer even aware of. The BC coast used to be thick with thirty-foot basking sharks, which slowly cruised the surface, feeding on plankton. So many boats collided with the sharks, or had their fishing gear snagged by the giants, that in 1945 the Canadian government began an eradication program. Boats outfitted with razor-sharp prows, looking like Phoenician warships, were sent out to run through as many sharks as possible. This went on for twenty-five years.

In 2008, the government initiated a program to help the sharks recover, but so far none has been found, and our experience of the waters of the Northwest has fundamentally changed.

But we haven't quite finished the job. Here and there, the grand and stirring influences still make themselves felt. It was easy to imagine ghost whispers swirling around the *Atrevida*, whose namesake is a Spanish corvette that spent several months sailing these very inlets in 1791. We were heading in the opposite direction, coming from the land to explore the coast, and we sought shellfish, not otters, but we still seemed connected to those earlier and larger missions, our fractalized adventure a tiny spur molded by the same waveforms that have shaped all natural and human history in this region.

And some of those connections were still intact. Not far north of us, the vertiginous Brooks Peninsula jutted nine miles into the Pacific. Its unassailable flanks deflected both the glaciers of the last ice age and human intrusion of any kind. "In a world shrunken by intercontinental air travel, 'lost worlds' still exist," the Royal British Columbia Museum's Richard Hebda writes. "One of these, virtually on our own doorstep, is the Brooks Peninsula." The peninsula harbors species dating back in an unbroken lineage to the Pleistocene. It's a treasure chest of DNA.

Whatever forgotten worlds lay waiting to be rediscovered would remain hidden to us that night, for we lost the sun long before we found the Nuchatlitz Channel. To call it a channel is generous. When the glaciers were done whittling the Nootka Island fjords, they tossed the whittlings at the edge of the sea. Those are the Nuchatlitz Islands, discarded in the tides like some giant child's game of jacks.

The full moon saved us. Without its wattage, we'd have been forced to spend the night at anchor. But soon the inky blackness was lit by a cosmic headlamp rising over Vancouver Island. It wasn't quite coincidental; the dates of our trip had been picked to coincide with the full moon, which provides the lowest tides of summer. But the clear skies were pure luck. We inched through the channel, praying that the GPS hadn't overlooked anything.

And then we spotted a fire in the distance. On the beach. Brian Kingzett crept close in the inflatable. Two members of the Nuu-chah-nulth tribe—whose ancestors had greeted Cook 230 years earlier—said, *Hey*. If they noted any irony in this visit of the *Atrevida*, they didn't show it. Sure, they knew Bob. No idea if he was around or not. Could you get to his place from here? Sure, but he lives around the other side of the island. You have to follow a shallow little channel. Go around, they told us, go around.

And so it was that at midnight, after nineteen hours of travel by car, ferry, and boat, Joth Davis and I found ourselves leaning over the front of the inflatable, figureheads in headlamps, calling out rocks as we led the *Atrevida* creeping through the reefs while the Pacific swell rolled in behind us. All clear in front—wait, too shallow. Back up. Rock! Oh, sorry, that's kelp. And so on.

At last we rounded a corner in the channel and there, breaking the surface glint, was Bob Devault's wooden boat, the *Nootka Rose*, tied up to his floating dock. We snugged the *Atrevida* alongside the *Nootka Rose* and piled out to collapse in Bob's living room and guest cabin and in tents on his lawn. I opted for a little berth on the *Nootka Rose*, but after those hours of hypervigilance, I couldn't sleep. I sat on the *Nootka Rose*'s deck and watched the moonlight play across the lagoon surface in white arcs and listened to the waves crash against rocks on the other end of the island. Occasionally something slapped at the surface or stirred in the night. I strained my ears, trying to pick up any revenants. But I was new here, and didn't know what to listen for.

THE ENGINEER OF
THE ESTUARY

SINCE OYSTERS LIVE in estuaries, you'd be forgiven for assuming an etymological connection. An estuary is, after all, an oyster-ary. It's a wonderful, but coincidental, echo. *Oyster* goes back to the Greek word for shell, which was almost identical to the word for bone, *os* being the root. (Think *osteopath*. Or *ostracize*, from the Ancient Greek practice of banishing people by secret ballot, shells being the original ballots.) *Estuary*, on the other hand, derives from *aestus*, the Latin word for the tide.

Yet the echoes don't stop there. In the dictionary it isn't far from *estuary*, that most fertile cleft of the sea, to the estrogen-drunk state of *estrus*, which derives from the Ancient Greek *oistros*, a state of frenzy. Another coincidence, perhaps, yet what drives the *aestus* but the moon, which also drives estrus, as every woman knows. And oystermen themselves are no strangers to the moon and tides, which rule their harvesting rhythms.

Whatever the etymology, the serendipitous mingling of the words in English gets the metaphysics just right. Estuaries are the nurseries of the sea, the safe and enclosed places where small creatures are born, and oysters provide much of that fertility.

An estuary is simply a place where a river meets the sea. Usually this collision forms some sort of bay or barrier island, partially enclosing the estuary and maintaining a mix of fresh- and saltwater. The Environmental Protection Agency recognizes 102 estuaries in the United States, including some of our most noted waterways: Narragansett Bay, Long Island Sound, Chesapeake Bay, San Francisco Bay, Puget Sound.

An estuary's importance lies in its productivity. We think of the oceans as highly productive habitats, teeming with fish, but vast stretches of ocean are aquamarine deserts. All ocean life, like all terrestrial life, depends on its primary producers—the organisms that capture the sun's energy through photosynthesis and use it to build their bodies. This energy powers the entire food web as animals eat the primary producers and each other. On land, plants are the primary producers, but in the water, the main primary producers are single-celled algae. Because they rely on sunlight, algae can live only as deep into the water column as light can penetrate.

In addition to sunlight, all primary producers need nutrients—the raw material for constructing and fueling their bodies. Carbon is the basic building block, endless quantities of which are available in the form of carbon dioxide. But nitrogen, phosphorus, and tiny bits of iron are also necessary. Terrestrial plants draw these from the soil, but algae need to get them from the water, and that can be a problem because a lot of ocean nutrients sink to the bottom as detritus. This is the great dilemma of algae: They must stay near the surface, where the light is, but their food tends to sink. In some parts of the ocean, there just aren't enough nutrients to produce much life.

Fortunately, these vital nutrients are steadily delivered to the ocean by the rivers of the world. Rain washes the nutrients out of the soil and the rivers carry them downstream—and into estuaries. This makes estuaries the marine equivalent of the richest farmland. They even get excellent sunlight by virtue of their coastal shallowness. And that's why estuaries are algae factories.

Just as rich food is good in small doses, harmful at high doses, so an estuary can choke on its own richness. Algae blooms can thicken a bay like filé powder in gumbo, blocking light and robbing the water of oxygen as the algae die and decompose, suffocating animal life in the process.

In a healthy estuary, this doesn't happen, because a host of creatures is waiting to eat that algae. Some algae get eaten by zooplankton, tiny animals such as copepods and krill, and some by fish called menhaden, but the star algae-consumers are shellfish. They are like living pool filters, complete with hard outer casing. Each day, the casing opens a fraction of an inch and the pump turns on. They pump water across their gills, straining out algae and other particles and expelling the filtered water. Unlike man-made pool filters, shellfish power themselves, maintain themselves, and even manufacture their own replacements.

All shellfish eat a staggering amount of algae, but none provides full-service filtration like the oyster. Oysters filter many gallons of water through their bodies every day, and they proliferate into extensive beds or reefs, depending on the oyster species.

Oysters begin life as tiny larvae that swim and drift in the currents, looking for a hard surface to attach to. They favor other oyster shells, a sign that the spot has been pre-tested for oyster needs. Each generation grows up on the shells of its living and dead elders. Soon a chaotic lattice of oysters sprawls across a bay.

All those pool filters keeping the water clear allow sunlight to penetrate to the bay bottom. And that allows sea grass to grow. Like terrestrial plants, sea grass uses roots to draw nutrients from the soil, so it can live only in bottomland that gets sufficient light and is stable enough for its roots to get a grip. The latticework of oysters fills both those needs.

The flourishing sea grass creates a marine meadow. Working in partnership with the oysters and any kelp that might be in the estuary, it provides a living baffle that absorbs wave energy and reduces shore erosion. The edge of this baffle is the breakwater of oysters, holding the land in place like a line of rivets.

We don't think of most marine creatures as needing shelter, but the need to escape predators is universal. Some use speed or sheer numbers to improve their odds; the rest hide. Sea grass and oyster shell provide some of the best structure in the sea. Juvenile crabs and lobsters hide in sea grass, as do molting ones. Fish of many species spend their early days lying low in the grassy meadows. Sea cucumbers and sea urchins graze the grasslands.

Those seeking even better shelter move into the oyster reef itself. More than three hundred species have been counted on oyster reefs. You couldn't design better habitat. Oysters literally make rock. It's no metaphor. All limestone in existence was produced by shell-making organisms. They are nature's elite infrastructure builders.

When an oyster dies, its shell often stays intact, but slightly parted. The generations of curved shells, all glued together, create a labyrinth of connected alleys and vestibules accessible to only the very small. Amphipods—tiny crustaceans that are one of the key links in the food chain between plankton and larger organisms—fill oyster reefs. Fish such as blennies and gobies lay their eggs in the vaulted sanctuaries of articulated shells. Mussels, anemones, barnacles, sea squirts, and tube worms all glom on to the outside of the reef, contributing their own filtration services. Mussel shell is thinner than oyster shell, but very useful; it's the plywood to oysters' concrete.

Soon larger fish colonize the bay to feed on the reef and sea grass communities. Many are species we value, including flounder and other flatfish, salmon, menhaden, herring, anchovies, striped bass, cobia, silver perch, spot, speckled trout, Spanish mackerel, sea bass, sea trout, eel, sheepshead, redfish, snapper, butterfish, blue crab, stone crab, shrimp, drum, and mullet. Shorebirds such as egrets and herons move in to fish the reefs at low tide, and large predators like porpoises hunt at high tide.

This is why ecologists often refer to oysters as ecosystem engineers. Oysters create the condos, streets, schools, restaurants, parks, and even the water treatment plants of thriving undersea communities, and the great conversation of life begins.

Eastern oysters are the ecological-service kings. They are large and fast-growing, the only oysters to form massive reefs—a Long Island lighthouse was even built on one—and can each filter fifty gallons of water per day. Olys are small and slow-growing, more likely to form beds than reefs, but they still filter twelve gallons of water daily per oyster and still form a unique ecosystem all their own. One of its most interesting residents is the harpacticoid, a tiny crustacean usually less than a millimeter in length. Harpacticoids aren't great swimmers. They prefer to hang out on the bottomland of estuaries, swimming up a few inches, particularly at night, to graze on algae.

Harpacticoids are the baby food of the sea—the first option for salmon, flatfish, drum, herring, anchovy, and many other species during their early estuarine life. Harpacticoids' slow swimming speed makes them easy to catch, and their small size makes them easy to swallow. They are also incredibly nutritious. Enzymes in their body allow them to create docosahexaenoic acid (DHA) and eicosapentaenoic acid (EPA), the two omega-3 fatty acids that are essential to the development of brains and nervous systems. We keep our brains sharp by eating salmon, and salmon build theirs by eating harpacticoids, which are much higher in EPA and DHA than similar prey. (In fact, harpacticoids are a focus of aquaculture research because fish fed harpacticoids grow faster and healthier than those fed typical fish-farm fare.)

Harpacticoids thrive in the kind of structured, three-dimensional habitat provided by oyster beds or eelgrass. In 2007 the Puget Sound Restoration Fund restored Olys to part of an intertidal beach in Liberty Bay, Washington, left the adjacent plot untouched, then commissioned Jeff Cordell of the University of Washington to assess the invertebrate population of each site. Cordell found significantly more invertebrates, including harpacticoids, on the Oly section. While many factors contribute to the collapse of salmon populations throughout the Pacific Northwest, loss of the oyster beds that nurture the food supply for juvenile salmon may well be one of them.

So yes, oysters are ecosystem engineers, but not just any ecosystem. They transform estuaries from algae factories into the most productive protein factories on earth. The transformation takes many paths. It goes from sunlight to algae to oysters. From sunlight to algae to harpacticoids to salmon. From sunlight to kelp to abalone to sea otters. From sunlight to eelgrass to sea worms to striped bass. And the best thing about this diversity is that more than a few of these paths lead to us.

IN SEARCH OF A VINTAGE FERRARI

O UR TRIP HAD been timed to coincide with some of the lowest daylight tides of the year because we needed as much intertidal real estate as possible to be exposed. (The very lowest tides of the year tend to occur in winter, in the wee hours of the morning, but we weren't up for that level of punishment.) Yet even these summer tides weren't necessarily cooperating with human schedules. Thus we found ourselves at six A.M., only a few hours after having collapsed in our sleeping bags, piling back aboard the *Atrevida* and the inflatable for the twenty-minute crossing to the fjord where Brian Kingzett had encountered his oysters.

We puttered back through the channel, which looked embarrassingly unchallenging in the light of day. The air was still, the world striped: a black band of conifers beneath a white line of fog lit by an invisible sun, then above the fog the dark hills topped by the robin's-egg sky, all reflected in the mirrored surface, as if we were boating through the alternating bands of yin and yang of an I Ching hexagram. Even the rocky islands we passed at low tide were striated in white, black, brown, and green, revealing the zonation: The white barnacles, at the top of the tide line, needed to be underwater for just a few hours each day; the black mussels could take a mix of wet and dry; while the brown and green seaweeds, near the low-tide line, could endure just a few dry hours.

Otters were everywhere. It's hard to accept that a species is threatened when you see dozens of them floating on their backs on the surface like Hollywood moguls in their pools, brandishing clams instead of cigars. Some seemed to still be snoozing in the kelp beds, which they use to anchor themselves while they sleep.

We emerged from the shelter of the Nuchatlitz Islands and cut across the open waters of Esperanza Inlet with the raw Pacific screaming in from the west. It became clear why all organisms on that coast, from shellfish to human, choose to live in the nooks.

We nosed into our particular nook, Port Eliza Inlet,

named for Lieutenant Francisco Eliza, first to explore it in the 1790s during the brief Spanish occupation of Nootka Island. The Spanish lasted on the BC coast just long enough to give its place-names a peculiarly Latin flair: Malaspina Inlet, Hernando Island, Cortes Island, Quadra Island, Esperanza Inlet, and so on. Port Eliza Inlet looked like a wide, slow river cutting through the mountains, and indeed, twelve thousand years ago it had been a river of ice, carving its channel down through the bedrock until the world warmed, the river melted, and eventually the seas rose to fill the groove. A classic fjord.

Despite our best efforts, we'd missed low tide by an hour. Olys tend to cluster low in the intertidal zone, where their exposure to air is minimal. If our oysters were still there, they'd already be submerged. Several miles up the inlet, Kingzett steered the inflatable near the first of the pocket beaches, and we dangled our heads over the side, noses pressed as close as possible to the glassy surface, trying to make out details on the shimmering bottom. Some black cobble . . . some white, barnacle-encrusted stones . . . then lots of shells—clam shells. We kept coasting along the shoreline, trying to spot some Oly patina among the whiter clams. But we saw only clam shells, mussels, barnacles, and more clams. Then, suddenly, the surface dropped a foot and the bottom color changed. "I got Olys!" Brian Allen yelled.

There they were: Olys, Olys, Olys. We kept drifting, and the Olys kept appearing. The mother beds had survived. Brian Kingzett allowed himself to smile.

Soon, Joth Davis and Brian Allen were pulling on wet suits and flopping over the side to commune with their favorite bivalve. Allen's head broke the surface. "Holy shit!" he called. "I'm snorkeling over a bed of Olys!"

Imagine somebody in the future stumbles upon one of the last cars in existence. It's a Ferrari, scattered in pieces, and isn't functioning, but a lot of the pieces seem to be in pretty good shape. This future dweller wants to put the thing back together, but he's never seen a working car and doesn't even have a manual. How can he go about it? Well, he could start tinkering, using his common sense, and if he's really handy, maybe he'll get it firing on a couple of cylinders. He'd roll across the land at five miles an hour and consider it a success, having no idea there are missing pieces he's never seen, and that such a car is capable of much more.

That's the situation facing those working to restore coastal ecosystems. Most of the systems still run, but decades of poor maintenance and occasional breakdowns have left them limping along. Few people can even remember what the systems are capable of.

If you wanted to restore a vintage Ferrari and you couldn't find a manual, the first thing you'd do is take a look at another Ferrari of the same model. When Brian Kingzett met Betsy Peabody at that 2006 conference, what he was basically telling her was, "Hey, when I was poking around those fjords, I came across a 308 GT in excellent condition."

The ecosystem of Vancouver Island is, for now, still firing

on all cylinders. Its intertidal zone is a biological hot spot teeming with mussels, barnacles, oysters, clams, rock scallops, periwinkles, limpets, crabs, sea stars, sculpins, and seaweeds of all kinds. Pacific salmon still push up the rivers every summer. Black bears camp out on the beaches. Wolf pups splash along the shore. Eagles loiter in the Sitka spruce tops, and black crows scoop up clams and shatter them on the rocks. Offshore, the kelp beds are thick with rockfish and urchins. Gangs of sea otters cruise the watery alleys. Farther out, gray whales skirt the coast and packs of orcas hunt the kelp forests for seal.

Immersed in such a place, feeling it hum along, you start to feel bad for the sputtering ecosystems we call home. Then you start fantasizing about what it would be like to live amid such vitality all the time. Then you start thinking about how to make that happen.

That dream was behind Betsy Peabody's creation of the Puget Sound Restoration Fund, and it's been driving a fundamental change in the mission of many conservation organizations. The Nature Conservancy is a perfect example. Its old campaign, "saving the last great places," is what most people think conservation is all about. But its new focus is on ecological services—preserving the habitats that keep the world running smoothly. If it were saving a country, it would protect the farms and houses before worrying about the museums.

That dream was also how Joth Davis came to be involved in tideland restoration. From childhood, he had known the elegant vitality of a fully functional littoral world—and he hadn't needed to grow up in the middle of the wilderness to experience it. Joth's ancestors stepped off the *Mayflower*, liked what they saw, and didn't wander far. He was raised in the Cape Cod town of Osterville, which of course had once been Oysterville. Growing up there in the sixties, Joth lived on a salt pond right across from a little Native American midden. "At that time the river was filled with oysters," he told me. "And hard clams, soft-shell clams, blue crabs. And you know, it's so sad, because if you go back to those same ponds right now, they're choked with algae. It's unbelievable." Runoff from the expanding human communities suffocated the estuary.

Gathering oysters and digging clams as a kid, Joth, who still has the sun-bleached good looks of a beachcomber, got a taste for the coast. After college he was hired to participate in a conch study by Cary Matthiessen, who would become his mentor. Matthiessen, the brother of the writer Peter Matthiessen, was a partner in Massachusetts's Cotuit Oyster Company, the oldest in the United States. Soon Matthiessen decided to head out to Fishers Island, off the Connecticut coast, to start an oyster hatchery, and he took Joth with him. They were sharp scientists, and they created what is to this day the top oyster hatchery on the east coast. "We had oyster seed coming out of our ears," Joth recalled. "The irony was that we'd go to Cotuit a couple of times each summer to spread seed oysters over the beds, and the damn conchs would eat them all. The same animals we'd been studying! Conchs just love oysters."

In 1990 Joth went to Washington State University to

get his Ph.D. He got married, had children, and never left. "I was working on triploid oysters and was thinking, 'Boy, these things really grow well here.' Then some tidelands came up for sale, and I said, what the hell, let's start an oyster farm." Joth's oysters, called Baywater Sweets, are some of my favorites, a perfect mix of salty and sweet. Later he began consulting with Taylor Shellfish Farms on its hatchery projects. It was satisfying work, growing sustainable seafood in a stimulating place, but in the back of his mind he knew that some of the cylinders were still missing from that particular engine. What would it be like to get Puget Sound perfectly tuned again?

When Betsy Peabody began contracting with Taylor Shellfish to grow Oly seed for her restoration projects, she started working with Joth. After a while, they agreed that simply putting more Oly seed into the water wasn't the best approach. For one thing, hatchery oysters have a restricted gene pool that can water down the remaining wild gene pool. But fundamentally, lack of oysters was not the limiting factor for Oly recovery. Lack of habitat was. The remaining Olys were spawning plenty of larvae into the water, but those larvae weren't finding many places to settle. The favored Oly habitat—other Oly shells—was long gone, replaced by a muck that would suck any settling larvae to their doom. Re-create good habitat, Joth suspected, and the wild oysters will take care of the rest.

Before he knew it, Joth was standing in Liberty Bay on the deck of a barge, on loan from the U.S. Navy, spraying tons of Pacific oyster shell—purchased from Taylor

Shellfish—over the side with a water cannon to form a nice, firm layer of cultch on the bottom. And now here he was, three years later, bobbing in fifty-degree water on Vancouver Island to get some sense of what a fully functioning and long-established bed of Olys looks like.

Eventually Joth and Brian Allen pulled themselves back onto the inflatable. They'd seen enough to know that we had to come back *early* tomorrow. There was more to be learned about Olys in this inlet than possibly anywhere else on the planet, and they didn't want to waste even an hour of our precious few days. Things were looking good.

From the steering column of the inflatable, Brian Kingzett produced a silver flask. He kept it on board, he explained, for emergencies: "Say you're in the middle of nowhere and suddenly you knock the outboard off the back of your boat. First thing you do is find the flask, unscrew the cap, and take a slow drink. Then you figure out what the hell you're gonna do." This was no emergency, but it seemed like an appropriate use of the flask. He handed it to Joth, who raised it into the air. It gleamed in the sun, and Joth, standing in his shining wet suit and hood, looked like a knight who had just found the grail.

HOW TO KILL A BAY

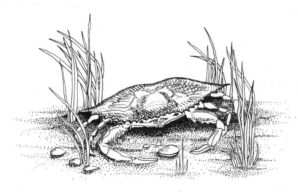

IN THE ESTUARY Hall of Fame, the place of honor is held by the "very goodly bay" conjured in this famous description: "Within is a country that may have the prerogative over the most pleasant places in Europe, Asia, Africa, or America, for large and pleasant navigable rivers . . . Here are mountains, hils, plaines, valleys, rivers, and brookes all running most pleasantly into a faire Bay compassed but for the mouth with fruitful and delightsome land." The bounty of the bay's waters was striking. "Neither better fish, more plenty, nor more variety for small fish had any of us ever seen in any place." Oysters lay "as thick as stones" on the bottom. The overall impression is of a shimmering paradise: "Heaven and Earth never agreed better to frame a place for man's habitation."

The writer is Captain John Smith, and the bay is the Chesapeake, the largest estuary in the United States. It's also probably the greatest natural oyster spot on earth, wide and shallow, putting virtually all its bottomland in the high-productivity zone. The very name is an Algonquin term meaning "great shellfish bay," and they weren't talking clams. Yet you'd be forgiven for not recognizing the modern bay in its 1608 description. The rivers no longer run most pleasantly, the fish are neither plentiful nor varied, and it's a challenge to find either an oyster or a stone on the sloppy bottom. It is no longer good habitation for shellfish or men.

If you wanted to destroy a bay, you'd have trouble improving on the three-pronged plan employed by the residents of the Chesapeake Bay watershed over the past three centuries. Step One: Rip out the trees and wetlands that act like a mesh reinforcement to the banks of the bay and its rivers, holding the soil together and trapping runoff before it enters the water. Colonial farmers got started on this task early, plowing their fields right up to the waterline and releasing great plumes of earth into the rivers of the mid-Atlantic. Over the following centuries, development filled in the wetlands.

Step Two in your destruction scheme: Remove the bay's protective lining of oysters. The Chesapeake's watermen certainly did that, although the bay was amazingly

The *Atrevida* slides into the fjords of Vancouver Island.
PHOTOGRAPH BY ROWAN JACOBSEN.

An Oly, up close and personal. PHOTOGRAPH BY ROWAN JACOBSEN.

The campsite in the Nuchatlitz Islands. The remains of a fish trap (underwater in this photo) run across the narrowest point on the channel. PHOTOGRAPH BY ROWAN JACOBSEN

Early morning in the Nuchatlitz Islands, a study in light and dark.
PHOTOGRAPH BY ROWAN JACOBSEN.

Joth Davis celebrates finding the Port Eliza oyster beds.
PHOTOGRAPH BY ROWAN JACOBSEN.

Betsy Peabody and Brian Kingzett in Port Eliza Inlet.
PHOTOGRAPH BY ROWAN JACOBSEN.

Did humans evolve in a coastal environment? Puget Sound Restoration Fund ecologist Brian Allen makes a compelling case.
PHOTOGRAPH BY BETSY PEABODY.

Expedition guides Brian Kingzett and Stephanie Richards of Vancouver Island University's Centre for Shellfish Research.
PHOTOGRAPH BY BETSY PEABODY.

The Nature Conservancy's Mike Beck counting oysters in the rain.
PHOTOGRAPH BY BRIAN KINGZETT.

Mike Beck (left) and the author on Pocket Beach #3. PHOTOGRAPH BY BRIAN KINGZETT.

Clam garden in the Gulf Islands, near the BC–Washington border.
PHOTOGRAPH BY MARY MORRIS.

Clam garden in BC's Broughton Archipelago. PHOTOGRAPH BY JOHN HARPER.

The Pinnacle Point cave in South Africa where, 164,000 years ago, early humans feasted on shellfish. PHOTOGRAPH BY CURTIS MAREAN.

The inside of the cave. PHOTOGRAPH BY CURTIS MAREAN.

Wild oysters recruited to a ReefBLK unit in Mad Island Marsh Preserve, Texas.
PHOTOGRAPH BY MARK GAGLIANO.

A ReefBLK "reef" in Mad Island Marsh Preserve. Note the sediment that has
accumulated on the inland side of the reef. PHOTOGRAPH BY MARK GAGLIANO.

resilient. In the 1880s, after more than a century of full-throttle assault, the Chesapeake oyster fishery was still the largest in the world, plied by thousands of watermen in sail-powered dredgers pulling in more than one hundred million pounds of oysters per year. Oysters formed reefs several feet high that broke the surface at low tide and even eviscerated the occasional ship. So many oysters lived in the Chesapeake that they filtered its entire volume every few days.

The twentieth century brought decline, but annual harvests of more than twenty million pounds were a given as recently as the 1960s and 1970s. Then the bottom fell out. Five million pounds in 1988, one million in 1996, and just a few hundred thousand pounds today—less than 1 percent of historical norms. If the harvesters of those oysters happened to notice the unique community of creatures making its living amid the reefs, they didn't bother recording it.

With the bay stripped of its natural capacities to block sediment and to cleanse itself, the coup de grâce could be delivered in Step Three: Install a battalion of sewer pipes, burying the estuary under a mountain of merde in all its forms.

The Chesapeake is an unusual bay. It drains a vast watershed of sixty-four thousand square miles, reaching into the states of Virginia, West Virginia, Maryland, Delaware, Pennsylvania, and New York, plus the District of Columbia. Yet 80 percent of it is less than six feet deep. The old joke is that if you fall out of a boat on the Chesapeake, stand up. It's basically a flooded river valley in a flat land. So while the area of the Chesapeake is huge, the volume is not. Yet it has to absorb the effluent of seventeen million people, thirteen million pigs, four million cattle, a hundred million chickens, and tons of fertilizer.

Hundreds of millions of pounds of nitrogen, phosphorus, and other nutrients pour into the bay from sewage treatment plants, suburban yards, and farms. This runoff clouds the bay and fuels the catastrophic algae blooms that now coat the Chesapeake every spring and summer. Algae have a seasonal life span; they soon die and decompose, a process that uses oxygen, leaving watery "dead zones" in which fish and crabs can't breathe. In 2007, the dead zone stretched almost the entire length of the Chesapeake and caused forty-five fish kills in the watershed, including seven thousand dead fish in Baltimore Harbor, twenty thousand dead in Annapolis's Weems Creek, and more than three hundred thousand dead in the Potomac.

Crabs are faring even worse. Today the "Maryland crab cake" is most often made with crabs from Asia, because the crustaceans immortalized by William Warner in his Pulitzer Prize–winning *Beautiful Swimmers* are now going the way of the oysters. Crab harvests collapsed in the 1990s. In 2008 the federal government declared the blue crab fishery an economic disaster, and Maryland and Virginia imposed strict harvest limits in an effort to save it. They would have restricted the harvest years earlier, but lobbying by the watermen stymied that effort.

For the crabs, the problems are lack of oxygen and

disappearing eelgrass. In addition to harboring most of the critters that crabs eat, and to being salad in itself, eelgrass produces oxygen and provides hiding spots for juvenile crabs and for adults during their vulnerable molting phase.

Unprecedented resources have been channeled toward saving the bay. In 1983, Pennsylvania, Maryland, Virginia, and the Environmental Protection Agency struck a historic agreement to tackle the two big problems: reducing the pollution going into the water and restoring the oysters that pull algae out of it. But by 2000, little progress had been made and Pennsylvania, Maryland, and Virginia agreed to put some numbers in place, aiming to reduce the amount of nitrogen entering the bay by 110 million pounds per year by 2010. As of 2008, with nearly six billion dollars spent on restoration efforts, they had managed to eliminate only 19 million pounds per year.

All the on-the-ground efforts by nonprofits and state agencies were being hamstrung by the feds. William Baker, president of the Chesapeake Bay Foundation, said that the EPA was "worse than missing in action. They have been a negative factor. They have not been enforcing the Clean Water Act. They have relaxed restrictions on air pollution, specifically on coal-fired power plants, and they've cut back on funding to states for things like sewage treatment plant improvements, and that's the low-hanging fruit when it comes to pollution." Officials decided not to reach for the higher fruit—farms and septic systems—because they didn't want to put a financial burden on individuals. Today there are more than fifty thousand inadequate septic systems in Maryland alone.

Meanwhile, the foundation's oyster restoration program grows millions of seed oysters in hatcheries and adds them to the bay every year. It has mobilized thousands of volunteers to do everything from rebuilding shorelines to participating in the oyster gardener program, where individuals and institutions with bay frontage receive seed oysters and grow them in protective cages until they are large enough to be planted in the wild bay.

In terms of galvanizing action for a noble cause, it's an incredible success story. But the sad truth is that since oyster restoration efforts began in 1994, the number of oysters in the Chesapeake has actually declined. That's right: After planting millions of baby oysters in the bay every year, running up a bill of sixty million dollars, we have fewer than ever. It's not that the programs aren't well planned or executed; it's simply the scope of the problem. The few oysters in the bay can't keep up with the nitrogen landslide. As fast as restoration programs add new oysters to the bay, the muck swallows them up. Even with all the work being done by the oyster restoration program, all the oysters and cultch added to the bay, suitably firm habitat is disappearing at an annual rate of 3.5 percent. Underwater videos of the bay bottom show a monotonous landscape of brown, lifeless ooze. "It'll always be beautiful," one former waterman said about the bay in a 2009 *Washington Post* article, "but there's nothing out there living."

New restoration efforts are starting to focus on constructing artificial concrete reefs that mimic the oyster reefs of old—structures that rise several feet off the bottom and provide lots of vertical habitat. These have had some success, but unfortunately most of the oysters that escape the muck get scarfed by cow-nosed rays or killed by diseases, which exploded in the Chesapeake in the 1970s and 1980s and helped engineer the final collapse of the oyster fishery. A healthy and extensive population of Chesapeake oysters would show more resilience to the diseases and might evolve resistance to them over enough generations, but the few survivors are too weakened by their environmental conditions to mount much of a defense.

After learning this history, you might assume that the handful of remaining wild oysters in the Chesapeake are protected. But you'd be wrong. With less than 1 percent of the oyster population remaining, the commercial harvest continues. The watermen are a romantic part of Chesapeake history, after all, and we wouldn't want to see that disappear. It's kind of like if we allowed a handful of loggers to keep hacking away at Redwood State Park in the name of tradition.

This is why few of the remaining oysters in the Chesapeake ever get to make more oysters. If the sludge and diseases and cow-nosed rays don't get them, the watermen do. The funny thing is that the very oysters being dredged by the watermen and brought to shore probably began their life in onshore hatcheries. It's an elegantly absurd system. Taxpayers pay the government to grow millions of seed oysters in hatcheries. These oysters are for the watermen, but, to make the game more sporting, we hide the oysters in the bay. Then we make the watermen wait a few months, and, for all I know, blindfold them and spin them around three times, before they set out to find the oysters. When they do, they get to haul them up and sell them back to us. Really, we could save money by cutting the bay out of the loop entirely and just letting the watermen fish for oysters straight out of the hatchery tanks.

We don't need an environmentalist to point out the insanity in the system; an economist will do. In terms of nitrogen removal alone, an oyster reef in Maryland's Choptank River was estimated to provide $181 of benefit per hectare per year. Over a ten-year period, that reef was worth $314,836—significantly more than the dockside value of the oysters. A separate study estimated that each hectare of oyster reef produces an average of $3,700 worth of commercial fish each year—again, far more than the harvest value of the oysters. Without even getting to the other ecological services provided by oysters, we can see that they are worth several times live what they are shucked. The oyster market can be served by oyster farms, which provide water filtration as a bonus.

Yet even if the oyster harvest stopped today, it might be too late to save the Chesapeake. Indeed, increasingly harsh harvest restrictions on oysters have failed to stem the hemorrhaging. The same loads of nitrogen and phosphorus seem to be causing worse dead zones than they used to. It's as if the bay is losing its last shreds of resilience. Like a living body, its systems will work to bring it back to a state of health, but only up to a point. Once the vital signs drop far enough, all the transfusions in the world can't turn things around. All they can do is slow the collapse.

We may have killed the Chesapeake. It is no longer the body of water that John Smith encountered and that Native Americans had been a part of for millennia. But in this horror story, death is not the end. For something seems to be stirring in the murky depths of the bay, and while you couldn't quite call it alive, you wouldn't be far wrong to call it the living dead.

It starts with that sediment flowing into the Chesapeake. Sediment has been an issue in the bay since the first colonists plowed their fields, but that sediment was mostly dirt that quickly sank out of solution. It didn't stay suspended in the greater bay and create the greenish-brown soup we see today.

Modern sediment includes vast loads of organic matter from animal farms and wastewater treatment plants, which feed the algae blooms that clot the bay each spring and summer. But algae aren't the only cloud. If they were, then visibility in the bay would improve during times of low algae activity, such as during dry spells. But that doesn't happen.

Why not? No one knows for sure, but the current best guess is that the ghosts of algae past are exacerbating the problem. So many nutrients have been flooding the bay for so long that in addition to the living algae, there is a constant haze of dead cells in the water. These cells, being mostly water themselves, don't sink easily. Oysters would normally remove them along with the living algae, but the oysters aren't there. Instead, the cells stick to the fine particles of sediment steadily flowing into the bay, forming agglomerations that drift about endlessly. Even when they do settle to the bottom, they are so light that the slightest agitation from storms or passing boats stirs them up again. This semi-biological, undead plasma is now permanent, and the formerly bright-eyed bay continues to cloud like a cataract.

All that living and once-living matter suspended in the bay is, in a sense, the very same material that once comprised the bodies of grasses, oysters, crabs, and other benthic life. As new material entered the bay, it was quickly sequestered by these organisms. Now, it is almost as though a neutron bomb has atomized them and suspended their bodies in a fine bisque. According to Jeremy Jackson, a professor of oceanography at the Scripps Institution, "Today Chesapeake Bay is a bacterially dominated ecosystem with a totally different trophic structure from a century ago." This trend, which Jackson calls "the rise of slime," is occurring along coasts all over the world.

We seem to have our choice of two Chesapeakes, each one self-reinforcing in its own way. We can have a pre-evolutionary microbial miasma, or we can have the dazzling diversity that John Smith encountered in 1608. Smith didn't tend to dwell on nature in his writings, so we can only imagine what that Chesapeake was like, but it must have been the kind of place to make a person settle down and never leave.

While the Chesapeake is the poster child for failing oyster ecosystems, it's far from alone. The Gulf of Mexico is now the front line in the battle. It used to be an oyster paradise to rival the Chesapeake. Oysters were so prolific in its shallow waters that drifting shell from dead oysters formed low islands in the wetlands. As old shell was crushed in the waves, it produced the beautiful beaches of the Gulf. In the soft sands of the area, the oysters were especially vital because their reefs were the main protection for the banks. The formation of those reefs thousands of years ago was what stabilized that coast in the first place. Once we'd overharvested the oysters and dredged the shell for road material, nothing was left to prevent storm surges and boat wakes from chewing away the banks. Today alarming chunks of Texas and Louisiana collapse into the water each year.

Like the Chesapeake, the Gulf of Mexico is now plagued by an annual dead zone, which extends three hundred miles beyond the mouth of the Mississippi into once prime shrimp areas. Even Hood Canal, a formerly pristine fjord on Washington State's Olympic Peninsula and the site of Joth Davis's oyster farm, has succumbed to a crippling dead zone. Around the world, more than four hundred dead zones are recognized, and they are doubling in size every decade.

Mike Beck and Rob Brumbaugh, who spearhead the Nature Conservancy's Global Marine Initiative, are some of the first scientists to attempt an estimate of worldwide oyster stocks. Their conclusions aren't pretty. Oyster populations are either gone entirely or failing badly in North America, Europe, and Asia. Only in parts of Australia and South America are they holding their own. Data for Africa aren't available. Overall, say Beck and Brumbaugh, about 85 percent of oyster populations have been lost. They have been extirpated entirely from 37 percent of their former bays. That's even worse than coral, the other endangered ecosystem-forming marine organism. If coral is at Code Orange, then oysters—and all the marine life that relies on them—have been at Code Red for decades if not centuries. If they go, so does our last hope of holding on to a world that may soon seem purely mythic in its abundance.

WHY HERE AND NOT THERE?

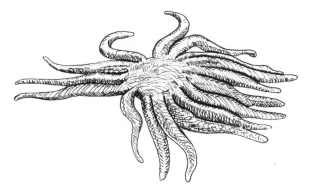

W E WEREN'T THE only mammals interested in the Port Eliza beaches. At low tide, black bears would descend on every beach in the inlet, rolling rocks to eat the blennies and crabs hiding underneath. In fall the bears rely on the chum salmon that spawn in the streams that had made these beaches, but the rest of the year they know that the easy protein is to be had on the beach. I wondered if, in addition to the crabs and fish, they ever ate the oysters or clams. I've seen footage of Alaskan brown bears digging clams. They lean on one paw and use the other to scoop out sand until they reach a clam. Then they pull out the clam and either work a claw between the shell and pry it open, or simply stomp on the shell to break it. It's almost always female bears with cubs that dig clams.

Some of the black bears on our beaches were juveniles that spooked easily, but there were also a few heavy-weights that looked unimpressed by anything that wasn't them. We also saw moms and cubs. Generally black bears don't mess with people, but there are reports of attacks, including one in BC in 2008 in which a bear swam across a river, climbed into a man's boat, and mauled him.

Our routine was to stagger out of cabins, tents, and boats at the crack of dawn, grab granola bars and coffee, motor through the fog to the large crescent-shaped beach at the head of Port Eliza Inlet, shoo the bears a little farther up the beach, and get to work. We worked in teams, one person tallying oysters and the other keeping an eye on the bears. We focused our efforts on the beach at the head of the inlet because it was several times larger than the pocket beaches along the sides. It had, we estimated, more than a million Olys on it, an astonishing sight.

Working from a protocol Joth Davis and Brian Allen had designed for studying Olys in Puget Sound, we needed to gather a lot of data. How many oysters were on these beaches? How dense were they? Where on the beach did they like to be? How big were they? How old? How many generations? What did they set on? (Rock? Wood? Shell? Each other?) What did they eat? Who ate them? Were they intertidal or subtidal? Ultimately, we needed to know why the oysters were still here. What was different about this place? And did other places used to be like this?

Some might find the minutiae of oyster surveying less than stimulating, but I thought it had a nice Zen quality. You take a quadrat, which is a one-quarter-square-meter frame of PVC tubing, empty your mind of intention, and haphazardly fling the quadrat over your shoulder in an attempt to embody true randomness. Wherever the quadrat lands, that's your study sample. You sit on the wet tideflat with your clipboard, hoping that your foul-weather gear has no leaks and that you can complete your survey before the tide covers you, and you count everything within the quadrat: oysters, mussels, barnacles, snails, crabs, algae, wood, rocks, silt coverage, and so on. You note what the oysters are setting on and how many of them are dead. The Zen part is that your quarter meter of tideland quickly becomes your world. The less-Zen part is that every now and then you remember the hungry bear hunting protein a hundred yards behind you.

That was the routine for us grunt laborers. Joth and Brian were after smaller game. Armed with plankton pumps and algae presses, they set out to learn about the microscopic world of Port Eliza. By first filtering water through a 300-micron screen, and then filtering the same water through a 75-micron screen, they could trap everything in the range of 75 to 300 microns—Oly larvae.

Joth and Brian also hung oyster shells from sticks with fishing line and stuck them in the mud at the low-tide line in the hope that, as the water covered them, oyster larvae might set on them. They installed plastic mesh fyke traps to catch fish and other high-tide visitors. Unlike any other ecosystem, the intertidal zone has an abrupt shift in demographics every six hours. While it was practical for us to observe and collect oysters at low tide, we needed to understand their high-tide life, too.

Back on the *Atrevida*, Joth and Brian took salinity readings. During our days in the inlet, we recorded salinities ranging from a fully marine 31 parts per thousand (ppt) to a brackish 15 ppt, depending on the tides, the winds, the rain, and even the depth of the sample. Freshwater is less dense than saltwater, so if it doesn't get thoroughly mixed, it will float on top. Sometimes this is dramatically visible. The conifers in temperate rainforests are full of tannins, compounds that act as preservatives and insect deterrents, and a hard rain can leach those tannins out of the soil and wash them into the inlets. "I've been diving in crystal clear thirty-two ppt inlets near streams," Brian Kingzett recalled, "and above me was a ceiling of rippling brown tea."

Joth and Brian Allen also put the Van Veen grab to work. The workhorse of benthic ecology, the Van Veen grab consists of a derrick that holds a pair of excavation scoops on a chain. You swing the scoops out over the side of a boat, release the chain, and the scoops plunge into the water. When they hit bottom, they automatically close on a scoopful of sediment, which can then be winched back into the boat and sampled for invertebrates.

All this data, we hoped, would help us develop our

snapshot of a system that could support healthy Oly populations. From the remnant populations in Puget Sound, the Washington Staters had developed a definite idea of what the oysters liked. Many Puget Sound Olys survive in those man-made lagoons created by oyster farmers a century ago, or in other structures that mimic tide pools. Some populations endure where freshwater or tidal seeps wash over them. And they persevere by piling onto shells wherever they can.

By those criteria, this was anything but prime Oly territory. Without any lagoon-like feature, the oysters seemed worryingly exposed to the elements. They were also vulnerable to predators and nonnative competitors, including Manila clams, varnish clams, and Pacific oysters. Their distribution was patchy, with solid Olys in one square meter, none in the next. They were piled in ridges that paralleled the shore, and a creek cut right through the middle of the beds. In the creek channel was nothing but rock. And where was the base layer of shells? Most of these oysters were clinging to stones; we saw no sign of their ancestors. "There's no oldness here," Brian Allen observed. Like citizens in *Logan's Run*, the older oysters and their shells seemed to get vaporized in the prime of life. The population was holding its own, but it was staying just a few generations ahead of oblivion.

For comparison, we sought another inlet on the other side of the Nuchatlitz Islands. Mary's Basin, the inlet with the bottleneck where Brian Kingzett had busted his propeller fourteen years ago, was rumored to hold the largest

Oly population of all. "I've had four different people tell me that Mary's Basin is the best place to find Olys," King-zett said. "I didn't see any when I did my survey in there years ago, but maybe the tide was too high at the time." We wouldn't be able to get in there at low tide either, due to that bottleneck. The basin is shaped like an hourglass, with one end open to the sea. As the tide rises, that end fills, but then the water must squeeze through the narrows to get to the inner basin, which creates a backlog. The outer basin rises higher than the inner basin, creating a white-water rapid as the tide flows down to the inner ba-sin. Then, as the tide falls, the flow is reversed: The inner basin holds on to the water, which pours out through the bottleneck. It's impossible for a boat to run these water-falls, but at mid-tide, when the two basins are equal, it's a smooth ride.

Once the tide rose at the head of Port Eliza Inlet, we boated to Mary's Basin. The two basins were nearly level, and we glided easily through the thirty-foot-wide constric-tion. We found ourselves in a stunning refuge, a perfectly contained bowl of green slopes and milky-blue water. Three bears nosed through the grasses at the head of the inlet, and an eagle arced overhead. Any oysters were under six feet of water, so we pulled on wet suits and snorkels and fanned out on an oyster safari.

Visibility sucked. I dove through the milk and found a bottom littered with clamshells and sand. I could see only a few feet of ground before having to return to the surface for another gulp of air, and in perhaps a half hour of snorkeling I found nothing. The other four snorkelers agreed: Not a single oyster lived in Mary's Basin.

Which made no sense. "If you wanted to design something as close as possible to an Oly pond from turn-of-the-century Washington State, this would be it," Brian Kingzett mused later. "Remember the color of the water? You see that a lot in these British Columbia tidal basins. They're like phytoplankton furnaces—a really high rate of productivity. You get this mixing at the entrance twice a day, with a surge channel coming into the basin. It gets supercharged with new ocean nutrients. There's fresh water coming down. And then it stratifies because it's got a reduced tidal cycle. The sun hits it, it warms up, and that phytoplankton can really cook."

Great food, reduced tidal amplitude, no disturbances—from a Puget Sound perspective, Mary's Basin should have been an Oly paradise. And from the reports, it once had been. Now the Olys were gone. Why? No one knew, though Kingzett had a theory. "Bob did say that last winter he flew in on a floatplane and saw two hundred otters in Mary's Basin riding out a storm. The physical movement of two hundred otters digging clams could bury oysters in soft sediment."

Meanwhile, Olys were clinging happily to the shelterless shores of Port Eliza Inlet.

Clearly, we had a lot to learn.

In the evening, sore and soaked, we gathered around the table in Bob Devault's house, passed a bottle of Canadian whiskey, and batted around the day's findings. It was science at its best, a freewheeling roundtable of ideas as we tried to make sense of what we'd seen in Port Eliza:

BRIAN ALLEN: The inlet had this big drop-off at the head. It looked like a dozer is pushing that material out. You've got these very steep and powerful drainages above the tideland. Those creeks don't stay in their channels from year to year; they move around. In the channel you've got absolutely nothing. No life—maybe a little algae on the edges. And then you've got nice, thick, dense, five-hundred-per-square-meter Oly populations right next to it. During storms, as the creeks rise, that channel's going to inch over, and so is the lifeless zone. And in three or four years' time you're gonna have dense oysters again where the channel used to be.

JOTH DAVIS: Exactly. Anywhere you see significant freshwater, a stream channel, you see no oysters. But as soon as you get onto any gravel or shelf, you see Olys immediately, and sometimes you see carpets of them. It was extremely variable from low density to high density.

BRIAN KINGZETT: I would argue that they're maximizing the available habitat.

MIKE BECK: They were still spotty in places in there. I would assume that under better conditions they would be more abundant in the spotty places and probably covering a better range.

BRIAN A.: My impression of the beaches around here is that anything that existed more than five or six years ago is no longer there. Whatever we saw on today's beach is a product of the last five or six years. There's a lot of physical disturbance. And there's no soft sediment for old shell to stick around; it just gets pushed out. My thought is if we were to regularly watch this group, at some point they'd have a population crash because of the disturbance, and it would only take them two to six years to get back to the state we see today.

BRIAN K.: But here's the weird thing. It's been thirteen years since I was on these beaches, right? And when I was out there today, I had a freaky déjà vu moment. I was throttling up the boat when we were done, and suddenly realized that thirteen years ago I pulled off that exact beach and throttled up at exactly the same mark. And I realized that the windrow that we saw out there is the windrow that I photographed thirteen years ago. Those populations are exactly the same.

MIKE: What's the limiting feature, here and elsewhere?

BRIAN A.: I've always thought, with the Oly in particular, that it's almost entirely habitat-driven. You'll see what should be a pretty good spot for them—there's larvae in the water column, food isn't limiting—yet for some reason you can't find an oyster on that beach. And then you've got other places that may not be the most hospitable, but there's some consistent feature that has high densities of naturally recruiting oysters, maybe two or three year classes. There's some piece of the puzzle that's just not revealing itself.

BRIAN K.: These are unusually cobbly beaches in Port Eliza; that might be a key to survival. I've walked every beach in Clayoquot Sound, Nootka Sound, and Kyuquot Sound. I've found Olys everywhere, always in the same kind of spot. Much like the beaches we saw today, there'd be an overhanging beach, a little stream delta, quite often sandier than what we saw today. You'd have a fringe of eelgrass just below the low-tide line. And right at the border of this eelgrass, if there was any hard substrate peeking out of the mud or sand, there'd be Olympia oysters on it. But in the hundreds, not the thousands—maybe five per square meter, in just this narrow band. Which doesn't line up at all with what Willapa Bay or Puget Sound once had. That's what makes this place so fascinating.

BRIAN A.: You've got reasonable recruitment frequency. They're low enough on the beach to survive desiccation. There's a lot of freshwater. Something is deterring predators.

BRIAN K.: I have this theory. It's not really a scientist theory—more of an oyster-farmer theory. I had these two beaches in San Mateo Bay, right? And I was trying to grow Manila clams on them. One beach fell right off, like the ones we saw today, and one had a long, gradual run-up. And the one that had the long run-up got sea stars on it. It was like this sea star militia that ran down at low water and at high water came back up. A sea star's gotta spend most of the day hiding out in the subtidal zone, waiting to come up onto the intertidal where the main resources are. If they get caught out of the water, the bears and eagles get them. One day I took a pound of Manila clams out of one sea star. I hired Stephanie's boys and told them I'd give them a quarter for every sea star they caught. And they came back two hours later and I owed them forty dollars. It was like a vacuum riding back and forth on this little beach. But my other beach fell right off into sixty feet of water and didn't get many sea stars. So I started thinking that maybe it was a refugium from predators because it fell off so sharply that there was no low-tide habitat to sustain a population of predators. I wonder if that's what's happening up here.

BETSY PEABODY: But a lot of the places you find Olys in Puget Sound are flat beaches with freshwater seepage.

BRIAN K.: Maybe the freshwater is holding the predators back.

JOTH: Freshwater is critically important to Oly beds and their longevity. My own view is that the freshwater is the cue that tells the larvae to drop. The fresh floats on top of the salt. If you're a larvae and you're floating around, you want to get back to an Oly bed. Where do you go? What do you do? If you go up into the water column, you'll just get swept away. You've got to feed, yet you can't feed until you get up into the water column. Maybe you hit that freshwater on top and drop back down. What we really need to know is why Olys persist anywhere, not whether they're happy; simply why they persist—both temporal persistence and spatial persistence. To me that's the key.

BRIAN K.: They're still a tender animal. They're still susceptible to things like bad winters and drying out.

MIKE: If they're such a tender animal, how could they ever have been as abundant as they were?

BRIAN K.: There's a beach in Deep Bay where we've documented a five-thousand-year history of continual aquaculture use. And we've got a two-thousand-year-old midden that we excavated last year, and we didn't find a single native oyster. We hand-sifted fifty cubic meters of midden material and found lots of cockles, littlenecks, butter clams, but not a single oyster shell. This is one of the best beaches in the province for shellfish. My thinking is, what would be the first species to go if you had a large population? They think there were a couple of thousand people living there. The first shellfish to go would be the oysters. If I move my family into a new area, the first thing I'm going to harvest is the thing that takes the least amount of effort—the oysters. You don't even have to dig them. We're here on the assumption that this is an optimal situation for these animals, but maybe it's suboptimal. Maybe it's the raggedy edge of what managed to survive because it didn't receive all those anthropogenic impacts. So if you choose this as a design endpoint, you may be equally incorrect, because biophysically it's so different from those other places.

JOTH: I didn't come up here thinking that what we found here could be replicated in Puget Sound. What I did hope was that we could potentially glean a few hints of why these populations are persisting in these odd, restricted areas. So the question I still have is, why do Olys seem to persist in these places?

BRIAN K.: If there's been such a massive drop in the Oly population, maybe these populations up here are actually really significant on the global ecological scale because, relatively speaking, they're such healthy populations. Locally, nobody up here cares about these oysters; they're just a point of curiosity. But we might be sitting on something really special. So let me ask a different question, kind of a rhetorical one: Why do we care about Olympia oysters?

BRIAN A.: Well, I'll tell you why I care. It's the native species, which sounds like a simple answer, but it means that it's coevolved with all the other native species of this place. The environmental landscape has changed because of all the things that people do—introduce species, alter habitat, and so on. But if we think that function of a system is important, then we have to try to keep around as many things as possible that are part of that function. I'm not saying that a Pacific oyster can't do what an Olympia oyster can, or even do it better. Here's a species that's been part of the original equation. It's like we're going into the future with blinders on. We're never going to have a complete understanding of the way these systems work. But if we can keep as many pieces of the system around, maybe some day we can start to understand why they are important to it. I mean, they're providing forage and refuge space unlike any other native species in the intertidal. They reproduce in a way fundamentally different than any other oyster on this coast. Those are pretty fundamental reasons to keep them around.

MIKE: They really were an abundant ecosystem, and that matters. We've changed the architecture of the system around here so much that we have no understanding of what "natural" might be. And if we don't care, then we end up on this slippery slope. You can say that we're doing just fine with the shellfish that we have, or that we can manage it, but once you look at it from a broader perspective, you see all the mistakes we've made that haven't worked out. We've done a very poor job of maintaining these systems in a way that could actually sustain a livelihood. As soon as you start down that slippery slope, there really isn't a good endpoint, and there are too many examples where everybody loses, in the human community as well as the natural one. As for these particular populations, I'm more concerned than I was before I got here. If these are the best of what's left of the populations, then we need to manage these things a little better. We're really at the tail end of what used to be, at many places along this coast, a quite important ecosystem. Not just a species, an *ecosystem*.

BRIAN K.: Okay, so Willapa Bay, southern Puget Sound, San Francisco Bay, Barkley Sound had these phenomenal Oly populations. There was a period when this animal was prevalent enough that it actually created a stock resource. And then we came in and did our classic fishery thing, maximizing production, and pulled the populations right down—in a number of different environments. Now you can find the animals, but at a vestigial level. I can take you to almost any inlet in the sound and find you Olys, but I can't find you a carpet except in these few places. And that's my big question: How did Willapa Bay and Barkley

Sound have such large populations? What was different? Was it a regime shift in the system?

JOTH: Exactly. And the new system is so perturbed that getting back to that old system is impossible.

BRIAN K.: It could be that when you get down to a residual population, then they're just not kicking out enough larvae to overcome other factors. Once you get too low, you're never gonna get back. It's a matter of straight odds.

JOTH: That's the part that depresses me. We talk about Chesapeake Bay restoration efforts, we talk about Willapa Bay or southern Puget Sound. But habitats are so modified now that it will never go back to what it was. One of the big reasons is that you just don't have the larval supply to get you over those big humps.

BRIAN K.: That's why on the Chesapeake this year they said that the only way to achieve their recovery goals was wide-scale aquaculture. For the Chesapeake, that's a fundamental change.

MIKE: It's somewhat unfortunate that the Chesapeake has come to dominate a lot of the discussion. The thinking seems to be, "Either we'll succeed or fail on the Chesapeake and that'll be that." If you consider the handful of places that still have healthy shellfish populations, it's a short list of two or three main ones and ten at the most—globally! It's a really silly short list if you're actually trying to think about these animals on a larger scale. Where should we be doing these conservation efforts? For example, we never think about the Gulf of Mexico as a conservation opportunity.

But we're at the edge in the gulf, which is one of the last places left in the world where there's still a significant wild harvest—and where we're set to re-create the same patterns that have happened everywhere else. We're sending the system down as fast as we possibly can. But we'll still talk about the Chesapeake instead of actually doing anything in the places where there are opportunities.

BRIAN K.: No matter who you are, at some point you've heard about the Chesapeake and oysters. The Chesapeake failed; it's gone. They've spent fifty-eight million dollars trying to bring it back and have nothing to show for it. But now it's happening in Hood Canal, just across the border from here. There was that big funding announcement, but it's only 10 percent of what's actually needed, which is the Chesapeake all over again. And we've got another twenty thousand people expected to move into the watershed here in Baynes Sound. We have a little jewel. It's not a Puget Sound or a Chesapeake Bay, but it's a jewel. It's this tiny piece of water that's become a nexus of conflict between urban development and a very significant shellfish industry. We already have every warning sign you expect to see. We have failing salmon streams. We have this little ecosystem that's maybe five years away from being Hood Canal North. It's just moving closer and closer, this gradual degradation and failure of systems. Let's learn from that. Let's try to do something *before* it's on the brink, instead of when it's on the brink.

ABUNDANCE

LET IT BE said that although intertidal research makes for some brutal mornings, it also produces sweet afternoons of high-tide downtime. We dug for butter clams, which has the same kind of treasure-hunting magic as digging for potatoes. You chip through the dirt and unearth little hunks of gold. We did our best to reduce the populations of such exotic species as the Pacific oyster; the Manila clam, which was accidentally introduced from Japan in 1920 along with the Pacific oyster; and varnish clams, a recent Asian transplant that arrived in ship's ballast. We caught sole. We ate beach onion and pickleweed. We dropped a shrimp pot into a deep gully and brought up a Dungeness crab.

When it came to procuring seafood, the only animal in the vicinity that could give the sea otters a run for their money was Brian Allen. With wet suit and speargun, Allen plunged into the kelp beds offshore and emerged with a string of rockfish. He cut a six-foot strand of kelp so I could make miso soup with the fronds and Betsy could make pickles with the stalk. He popped limpets off their rocky purchases and grilled them in their inverted shells for the ultimate beach appetizer. "Brian was born in this environment and loves everything about it," Betsy said to me as we watched him work. "He gets the most out of what this place has to offer."

I knew the feeling of carefully cultivating food in a vegetable garden, and the thrill of cadging a few chanterelles from the woods, but I'd never experienced the profound abundance of seeing miles of wild food stretch before me. And it wasn't even salmon season.

I love the Pacific Northwest for its drama and its misty beauty, but I especially love it because for ten thousand years it has been a really good place for people to live. Evidence of that was all around us. Bob Devault led us on a hike to an enchanting beach, where we climbed a daisy-covered hill and watched the sun dip into the Pacific behind islets that harbored ancient burial caves. We asked Bob if there were any middens in the area. "You're sitting on one," he replied.

From Bob's land, we could look down a sinuous tidal canal and see a line of boulders placed centuries ago as a fish trap. The simplest fish traps are nothing more than a wall of rocks running across the mouth of a stream. The wall is exposed at low tide but covered at high tide, with enough room for fish to swim over the top. When salmon are preparing to make their upriver spawning run, they'll congregate at the mouth of a stream and wait for the seasonal rains to raise the floodwaters high enough to be navigable. As they wait, they tend to flux in and out of the inlet entrance with the tides. Other fish will also swim up inlets in search of food. The wall of rocks allows the fish to enter at high tide, but then traps the stragglers as the tide falls. All you have to do is scoop them up.

One morning I counted oysters on a pocket beach for an hour, working around a mysterious semicircle of rocks, each about the size of my head, before Brian Kingzett pointed out that this, too, had been a fish trap. Instead of blocking a river's mouth, this style of trap was built on intertidal beaches. Often multiple scooped walls would line a beach like a giant pachinko game. Fish moved up at high tide, eating oysters, clams, and other littoral denizens, then, if they lingered too long, got cut off by the scoops and

A river-mouth fish trap.

A beach fish trap.

beached as the water trickled out between the rocks. Bears had rolled some of the rocks out of place in their search for goodies, but the original shape was still apparent.

I hadn't expected to be working in such an anthropogenic world. The standard textbook story—that America was hacked out of a vast and virgin wilderness—began to seem flawed to me. This was a land that had been fully peopled, a land that had been altered, yet not ruined, by them. Working casually around those fish traps allowed me to get a tantalizing taste of what it must have been like. Their relationship to place was different from what even the most environmentally oriented of us know today. They weren't visiting the landscape. They weren't admiring the landscape. They *were* the landscape.

In the past few years a new understanding of this bond has emerged. The story starts back in July of 1995. About the same time that the Environmental Protection Agency was feeding billions of baby oysters to the cow-nosed rays of the Chesapeake, and Betsy Peabody was gathering her ideas for a new kind of nonprofit, Brian Kingzett was surveying the beaches of the Broughton Archipelago, jotting "anthropogenic changes to beach" in his log and wondering about the Bell 206 helicopter gliding low over the same coast. A year later, he came across the copter and its occupants at an old float camp called Dawson's Landing. The copter was in the service of a geomorphologist named John Harper, who had been contracted by the BC government to make an extraordinarily detailed map of the coast. Known as the ShoreZone Project (and now expanded to include the entire coastline from the mouth of Oregon's Columbia River to Bristol Bay, Alaska), the map could be used for everything from studying natural communities to

Brian Kingzett (back row, second from left) and John Harper (back row, third from left) meeting in 1996 on the float at Dawson's Landing. Photograph by Mary Morris.

contingency planning in case of an oil spill. Harper and Kingzett were working the same territory at the same time, taking advantage of the same low tides, but they were under contract to different ministries and had been unaware of the other's existence.

As part of the ShoreZone Project, Harper was shooting video of the coast. To get the meaningful detail he needed, he was flying just over the treetops at about a hundred meters. As the images of thousands of kilometers accumulated in Harper's subconscious, something began to tweak his pattern-recognition centers—something he would later call an "unnatural symmetry." An astonishing amount of coastline in the Broughtons and other islands seemed to have a neat row of boulders at the low-tide line. The boulders trapped sediment, forming terraces. From the ground the boulders would have been visible only on the lowest tides of the year, but from the air the line of boulders was obvious.

As a geomorphologist, Harper specializes in the forms created by geological processes, and he had never seen anything like this. The closest similarity he could think of were stone walls on the shores of Labrador that were bulldozed into place by sea ice. Could these also have been created by sea ice in the distant past?

On July 15, 1995, Harper had noticed a terrace on the shore side of one of the walls that was conveniently wide and flat, so he instructed the copter pilot to land on it. Then he examined the wall up close. It couldn't have been formed by sea ice. The boulders were of a similar size and were stacked neatly to form a sloping meter-high rampart that ran between two rocky outcroppings, loosely paralleling the shore and creating a sort of courtyard that was filled with whitish, crushed shell.

Harper knew of no natural force that would select only certain-size stones to make the terrace and then would assemble them to make such efficient use of the space. He was forced to conclude that he was seeing a man-made structure. But he had never heard of any such structure on the BC coast. Who would have gone to such trouble? And what would it have been for? He had no clue, but he started paying close attention, and his conviction grew as he finished mapping the Broughton Archipelago in the following days. Virtually every beach with a suitable topography was rimmed by such a structure.

Harper eventually counted 365 such terraces in the Broughtons, which together covered more than eight miles of coast. What kind of man-hours would be required for such an undertaking? If they were, indeed, man-made, then it was like stumbling on a lost Machu Picchu.

The white hash in the terraces was mostly shell, and after a bit of research, Harper suspected that the structures had been built to grow clams. Butter clams, the tastiest Northwest variety, nestle one to three meters above the low-tide line, and the structures Harper had examined maximized the real estate in that zone. Like all clams, butters burrow into the bottom for safety, extending a siphon for food and oxygen. They like to be buried about a foot deep. They don't do well in substrates that are too rocky or too compact, and favor a loose hash of small shell bits—just what Harper had seen.

Harper compiled his observations into a report for the BC Ministry of Government Services. His report, *Broughton Archipelago Clam Terrace Survey*, describes the construction of the ramparts and the "sand flat extending from the ridge into the middle intertidal zone comprised almost entirely of biogenic sand."

He was told by the experts that he must be mistaken; there was not a single record of any such structure in all the literature. "The archaeologists didn't think they were man-made features, but couldn't say they weren't," Harper later recalled in a *Vancouver Sun* article. "On the other hand, I, the geologist, didn't think they were natural features, but couldn't say they weren't. Conventional science had basically failed." Anthropologists had never heard of any such tradition among First Nations groups. Others pointed out the sheer mathematical unlikeliness of it. It would take a

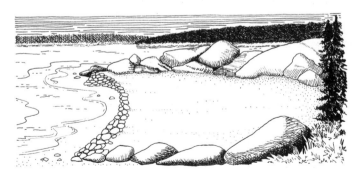

A clam garden.

very organized, stable, and sizable civilization to produce these walls. Was it remotely possible that such a major feature of Pacific Northwest native life had been overlooked by generations of trained anthropologists?

In a word, yes. Or so Harper believed. Yet for five years after his discoveries, he failed to find a single expert who had seen one or could confirm his belief.

Unbeknownst to Harper, a woman named Judith Williams had been investigating the very same features since 1993. A retired University of British Columbia fine arts professor with a home in the Broughton Archipelago and a lifelong interest in First Nations art and traditions, Williams was told by a Klahoose elder about the family's clam garden in Waiatt Bay. On a low tide in August 1993, Williams checked out the site and did indeed find a rock wall holding up a perfect terrace about ten feet above the low-water mark. This was no ancient ruin; the terrace was still going strong. "As we strolled the spouting, oozing, sucking terrace," she would later write in her book *Clam Gardens*, "it seemed a live thing . . . I was standing on an ancient living entity that could be destroyed in minutes by thoughtless bulldozing."

Williams reported her discovery to the archaeology branch of the BC Heritage Conservation Department. The department staff told her ancient clam terraces did not exist. Waiatt Bay had just been surveyed by *real* archaeologists, and they'd seen nothing of the sort. Further, anthropologists had been visiting the First Nations groups for more than a century, starting with the godfather of anthropology, Franz Boas, in the 1890s, and they'd never recorded any beach modification. Native peoples dug clams, sure, but that was it. What Williams must have seen, they told her, was a fish trap that had filled in.

Well, Williams knew a fish trap when she saw one, and this was no fish trap. Fish traps, like the ones I'd seen in Port Eliza Inlet, were placed higher in the intertidal zone and were generally near the mouths of rivers or streams. But she made no headway with the Heritage Conservation Department. Instead, pursuing leads from her Native informants, she kept working solo, visiting another clam garden and documenting her findings. In 1997, in part because of her alarm at how logging operations were encroaching on the site, she sent a report to the Heritage Conservation Department, but never received a reply. Williams believes it was because of her "off-topic qualifications." I suspect it was simply the black hole of bureaucracy.

But the conspiracy-minded might offer another possibility. Land use and Native rights are touchy issues in extraction-happy British Columbia. The last thing the province might want to acknowledge is that miles and miles of its coastline—the very beaches where they hoped to put in clam farms—might already *be* clam farms, as well as some of the most significant cultural artifacts in the province. As Harper told me, "The clam gardens ultimately will have an impact on treaty negotiations, although the extent is uncertain. The conundrum is that in English law, fences and walls have great significance with respect to property ownership. So once the features are acknowledged as man-made, the governments have a hard time denying that property rights should not prevail."

When the First Nations tribes were negotiating with the government in the early 1900s over which lands they could keep, they singled out certain clam beaches. Officials assumed that these were natural clam beaches; they didn't understand that the tribes were trying to hold on to places they had created over many generations.

In 2000, John Harper tracked down Billy Proctor, a man who had grown up in the Broughtons and had learned much from First Nations elders. Proctor not only confirmed that there were man-made clam gardens throughout the archipelago; he also showed Harper his own, which he had been cultivating for more than forty years. The small beach was still extraordinarily productive; it contained about ten thousand clams, half of them market-size.

Proctor's beach helped demonstrate what an appropriate term "clam garden" is, because, like a vegetable garden, a clam garden becomes more fruitful with careful tending. The first order of business, as with any garden, is to get rid of the stones, and that must have been the origin of clam gardens. As Brian Kingzett, a man who has dug more than his fair share of clams, speculated, "When you dig clams on a pocket beach, every time you turn over a rock, you roll it downhill. If you roll all those rocks downhill for a couple of decades, eventually you get a little berm at the bottom of the hill. And then that berm fills in with sediment and you've got a clam garden. An Indian clan would divide up a beach. That would be my family's section, that would be your family's section." Generations of humans perfect the wall, and generations of clams perfect the hash. The regular digging of the clams tills the hash, creating what one First Nations man calls a "fluffy beach"—clam heaven. If you're careful to harvest only the large clams and to replace any small ones you inadvertently dig up, your clam garden can last indefinitely.

Billy Proctor helped Harper realize that although knowledge of the clam gardens had never been conferred to the anthropologists, it had never been fully lost by the indigenous people. Harper shifted his investigation from the geological record to the human one. With the aid of an ethnologist, he met a hereditary chief of the Tsawatenok tribe of the Kwakwaka'wakw peoples. Chief Adam Dick (Kwaksistala) had learned English late in life and was trained to pass down the old knowledge. When asked about clam gardens, he remembered a four-verse song about children helping their mother, one verse of which refers to building a clam garden.

As it turned out, *lo xwi we*, the words for "clam garden" in the song, had been recorded by none other than Franz Boas in his unpublished dictionary of Pacific Northwest languages. He had translated them as "place of rolling rocks together." As Harper explained, "Boas never understood their function."

How had Franz Boas and all his heirs missed such a staple of First Nations culture? They may not have been at the right place at the right low tide. And they didn't, until recently, understand the gradations between hunter-gatherer and farmer. In Boas's mind, societies were either one or the other, and he believed the raincoast peoples were hunter-gatherers; he couldn't recognize that one could enhance the productivity—the edibility—of one's world without assuming the massive labor and responsibility that comes with a full commitment to agriculture.

Or it may have had to do with gender. The early anthropologists were all men. They had the same bias toward male culture as any other nineteenth-century man. They may have unwittingly considered what the First Nations men were doing more interesting—and the men were not digging clams. That was women's work. The men were catching salmon or hunting whales and seals. The men were fighting wars with other tribes or squabbling over property rights. That was the stuff that mattered. Who cared about shellfish?

Yet even George Vancouver noted the value of shellfish to the culture. Describing the village huts he saw in 1792 in Puget Sound, he wrote, "In them were hung up to be cured by the smoke of the fire they kept constantly burning, clams, mussels, and a few other kinds of fish, seemingly intended for their winter's sustenance. The clams perhaps were not all reserved for that purpose, as we frequently saw them strung and worn about the neck, which, as inclination directed, were eaten two, three, or half a dozen at a time."

To be fair, the anthropologists' bias toward men may have been partially because they simply had more access to them; cultural barriers may have prevented them from learning too much intimate knowledge from the women. Or, as Judith Williams points out in *Clam Gardens*, a more universal human trait may have been a factor: If you have a secret clam spot, why would you run and tell the visiting anthropologist about it?

Thanks to Harper and Williams, no one now denies that hundreds of miles of clam gardens were maintained by First Nations peoples for millennia, right through the coming of Europeans and European disease. And that matters. What's considered the wildest and most rugged coast in North America was actually a center of civilization, with a landscape that was both transformed by human beings and transformative upon them, providing such a profoundly fecund environment that its inhabitants, freed from the daily struggle for survival, found the time to develop the greatest artistic culture of the New World.

As Richard Manning points out in *Against the Grain*, it was not the first time this had happened:

Salmon show up in Cro-Magnon paintings—and their skeletons in Cro-Magnon sites—throughout Europe. Cro-Magnon people stayed in one place and had enough leisure time to paint, and they painted salmon because salmon were important to them. The rise of art much later among Northwest American Indians is unique among North American hunter-gatherers, suggesting something parallel in the two salmon cultures—a correlation between salmon, sedentism, and art. Fishing a migratory species allows all this. You simply stay put at streamside and the salmon come. Throughout the world, sites along rivers, seas, estuaries, and lakes show layers of shellfish and fish bones below (and thus older than) layers containing evidence of agriculture. These early sedentary people did not have to wander seeking game; currents, the habits of their prey, and the enormous productivity of marine systems like estuaries brought the prey to them. Agriculture did not arise from need so much as it did from relative abundance. People stayed put, had the leisure to experiment with plants . . . and were able to support a higher birthrate because of sedentism.

They also found the time, and the need, for some of the less appealing aspects of complex society. "Their songs were the equivalent of our paper records," Bob Devault, our expedition host, told me. "They had property rights nailed down solid. They owned all of their resources. There was lots of politics and murder and inheritance and bad blood." For example, John Harper was told by an ethnologist that the penalty for poaching another's clams would have been death.

They were, in short, a fully realized society, and more than a little of that society was fed by aquaculture. No one knows how many people lived on the raincoast before the Europeans introduced smallpox; it easily could have been ten times the currently accepted figure of one hundred thousand. Yet most people still think of the raincoast cultures as transitory hunter-gatherers who were somehow more primitive than the tribes using traditional agriculture elsewhere on the continent, a concept Judith Williams finds absurd: "The inhabitants of the most complex Native culture in North America did not wander aimlessly around in the rain hoping to trip over food. They planned to spend much of the wet winter indoors, around a warm fire, with enough dried salmon and smoked shellfish hanging from the rafters."

They didn't limit themselves to clam gardens and salmon traps either. They cultivated a variety of wild plants. They nurtured oysters where they could find them. They set up boulders in accessible places to attract mussel and giant barnacle sets. They selectively gathered seaweeds and shore plants. They stuck fir branches in the walls of their clam gardens and hung branches from wooden floats during the herring spawn to catch roe, which they would dry—caviar all year long. They ate like kings.

As did we. Sitting on Bob Devault's deck, polishing off his oysters, which hung from rectangular wooden floats virtually identical to those used centuries ago to catch herring spawn, I got an excellent sense of what it must have been like to live in an edible world.

And it wasn't just the First Nations who had lived well in this place. That evening, while leafing through a history of Vancouver Island's west coast compiled fifty years earlier, we stumbled upon a passage about Port Eliza Inlet: "Acres of native oyster beds occur at the head of the inlet, from which thousands of sacks were once shipped to

Vancouver and Seattle . . . Now they are free to anyone who wishes to gather them."

Thousands of sacks? This was no pristine inlet. The oyster beds had been plundered for decades. Yet they survived. Clearly, Olys had a long and productive association with a variety of creatures in the area, including *Homo sapiens*.

And that got Betsy Peabody thinking. "For me," she said to us as we sat around the table, "one of the main reasons for coming here was to get a glimpse of what it was like in Puget Sound a hundred and fifty years ago. I had a vision of the largest undisturbed native oyster beds that you could find. That's what we wanted to map and characterize and assess. I find it incredibly interesting to see that it's not an undisturbed system. In Port Eliza there's active logging, felled mountainsides, bundles of logs being rolled down while bears are foraging on the beach. And the oysters are still there—unlike Mary's Basin, which seems more remote. So I'm having to change my vision. It's not an undisturbed system. There's a lot going on up here. There are resources that are here for the taking— because we're human beings and that's what we do. Olympia oysters are among them. Trees are among them. So I recognize this as being more applicable to Puget Sound, not less. People have been living and eating here for a long time. So what we're trying to re-create is abundance—the kind of abundance that supported an early industry."

When you have enough abundance, then the old schism we have grown so used to—natural areas and civilized ones—simply disappears. That was what Betsy wanted to restore, that numinous sense of being in the midst of un-limited natural bounty. Opening piles of oysters or smok-ing pink slabs of salmon over a fire, you come unstuck from time. You stop struggling to impose meaning on your world, because meaning is implicit in everything you do. The peoples of the raincoast were some of the last to luxu-riate in such a world, but it is an old and universal draw. In fact, according to a new generation of scholars, that mag-nanimous coast may be what lured us to the New World in the first place, what made the journey possible. It's to that idea that we now turn.

AMERICA'S FIRST BANQUET

Here's a fun winter activity. Dress yourself in furs and deerskin boots. Fashion a spear from wood and set a stone point into the shaft. Make a second one, just in case. Now take some elephants from your local zoo and turn them loose in the ice fields of Alaska. Give them a one-week head start, then go hunt them. Bring some friends to help, but also bring your kids, your parents, your great-uncle Irving, and your pregnant sister-in-law. Object of the game: to see how long the group can survive.

If only this little activity had been forced on America's previous generation of archaeologists, then the past century's reigning theories about the peopling of the New World might have been different. For it was these archaeologists who developed the "Clovis-first" model we learned in school, which went something like this:

Thousands of large stone spearheads of beautiful workmanship have been found at dig sites throughout North America. The first of these was found in the desert near Clovis, New Mexico, in 1932, thus the entire style came to be known as the Clovis point, and its mysterious makers were dubbed the Clovis people. The size of the Clovis points—not to mention the fact that they were occasionally found within the ribs of bison and mammoth skeletons—made it clear that they were for big-game hunting. By dating the layer of sediment around the artifacts—and later, using radiocarbon dating—archaeologists determined that the Clovis sites were as much as thirteen thousand years old, making them easily the oldest signs of human presence in the Americas. In the 1930s, the establishment still believed that man had been in the New World for only a few thousand years. But the Clovis evidence overturned this.

Particularly compelling was the age of the artifacts.

Everyone agreed that the first Stone Age explorers must have come to the New World over a Bering land bridge. Currently the tips of Siberia and Alaska are separated by the Bering Strait, fifty-six miles of hundred-foot-deep waters. But during ice ages, a number of which have occurred over the past million years, a vast amount of water is trapped in glaciers, rather than in oceans, which lowers sea levels. In the most recent ice age, which peaked about eighteen thousand years ago, sea levels were hundreds of feet lower than they are today. Both the Bering and Chukchi seas, which separate Asia from North America, were laid bare, part of a thousand-mile-wide, relatively flat plain known as Beringia. "Land bridge" implies some sort of causeway, but Beringia was huge. As the world began to warm again, the glaciers thawed and the seas rose, until approximately thirteen thousand years ago Beringia once again disappeared beneath the waves.

So the timing looked perfect for Clovis hunters to have pursued mammoth and other big game across Beringia, through Alaska and Canada, and down into the rest of North America just before the watery door slammed shut between the continents. Even better, the fossil record showed that most of the big game in the New World—the mammoths, giant sloths, camels, horses, dire wolves, and so on—went extinct right about then. We came, we saw, we conquered.

There was only one problem with this theory, and it was a mile-high wall of ice. All that water that *wasn't* in the sea was piled on top of Canada and the northern half of the United States in titanic glaciers that stretched from coast to coast. Nothing could live on this lifeless sheet cake. Nothing could cross it. Stone Age nomads might schlep their way across Beringia (which was ice-free, thanks to sparse precipitation), but then they'd be stuck in Alaska until the Ice Age ended and the glaciers disappeared, which did not allow them to sprint down to New Mexico in time to leave their stone points in a Clovis mammoth.

This problem was "solved" by new geological models showing that retreating glaciers might have exposed a 2,500-mile ice-free corridor to the east of the Rockies connecting Alaska and the Great Plains. Although no human signs of any kind had been found in the corridor zone older than 10,500 years, nor any signs of plants or animals older than 11,000 years, for decades the ice-free corridor stood as the best idea anyone could come up with.

Eventually a few heretics dared to point out that chasing mammoths across thousands of miles of Arctic latitudes might be really, really hard. It seemed difficult enough for a few strong hunters to accomplish, but by definition, this had to have been a journey made by a reproductive and genetically diverse population over multiple generations. ("Come on, kids! Only thirty miles to go today. Get up, Uncle Irving, no time to be napping in the snow.")

Well then, responded the Clovis crowd, *you got a better idea?*

As a matter of fact, somebody did.

In 1969, a grad student at BC's Simon Fraser University named Knut Fladmark uncovered some stone tools at a site on BC's Queen Charlotte Islands that turned out to be eight thousand to nine thousand years old—not old enough to undercut Clovis, but old enough to get Fladmark thinking. The Queen Charlottes are among the most far-flung patches of North America, a good fifty miles from the BC coast and perhaps two hundred miles north of Nootka Island. They are the other half of Wrangellia, Vancouver Island's long-lost twin. And Fladmark thought that if people were way out on the Queen Charlottes nine thousand years ago, they might also have been there much earlier, when sea levels were lower and travel between many BC and Alaska islands would have been much easier. Could they have lived up and down the coast?

Fladmark was familiar with the Pacific Northwest. He knew how successful the coastal peoples had been for millennia, living off the resources of the northern Pacific. And he dared to propose that the first Americans might have come down the northwest coast in boats.

The establishment was unconvinced. Where were the sites to prove it? Where was the boat technology? And how could people have navigated thousands of miles of coastline that was one long calving-iceberg death zone?

The sites must be there, Fladmark countered, but they would be found along the coastline of, say, fourteen thousand to eighteen thousand years ago—and that coastline was now miles out to sea under several hundred feet of water. You wouldn't just happen upon them by accident.

Even if you knew what to look for, they'd be very difficult to find. This is a vital point not just for Fladmark's argument but also for all prehistory; there must be a ring of Atlantises around the world marking human coastal settlements during the Ice Age.

Since the 1970s, a midden of evidence has steadily piled up in support of Fladmark's theory. The DNA of grizzly bears on the islands of southeast Alaska, just north of BC, show that the bears have been evolving in isolation for tens of thousands of years. That means the bears were living on that coast right through the Ice Age, which they could not have done if it were buried under a mile of ice. The area had been habitable for bears, and big enough to support a breeding population, which meant it was habitable for people, too. Carbon dating of bear, fox, and caribou bones found in caves on BC islands show that animals have lived in the area in an unbroken lineage for at least fifty thousand years, refuting the old notion that they recolonized the area from southern regions after the glaciers melted.

Samples of coastal sediment laid down sixteen thousand years ago have yielded pollen and insect fragments that indicate a temperate land stretching from Beringia down to the Washington coast. A few years ago, archaeologists pulled up twelve-thousand-year-old pine tree stumps from 476 feet down in the Hecate Strait, the stretch of water between the Queen Charlotte Islands and the BC mainland—an ice-age forest. Another research team has found that edible shellfish were abundant along the coasts of thirteen thousand years ago. As they put it in their article "Quest for the Lost Land," "During the last ice age, early groups traveling along the northwest coast of North America would have seen coastal plains stretching over 100 kilometers as far as the eye could see, where now rough seas preside. They could have lived adjacent to productive estuaries and shellfish beaches now buried." The glaciers touched the coast here and there, but in between were many refuges easily reached by hopping from beach to beach in boats.

Was the technology available? Absolutely. After all, humans had reached Australia by boat forty thousand years ago. (Even *Homo erectus*, our not-so-evolved ancestor, was somehow crossing miles of open ocean in Indonesia nearly a million years ago.) In the 1990s, archaeologists confirmed that people in Japan were making twenty-mile water crossings at least thirty-two thousand years ago. We can assume that by sixteen thousand years ago boats were old news in northeast Asia. They probably resembled the umiak—sealskin hulls stretched over wood or bone frames—used by today's Inupiat. And those early mariners would have been just as comfortable in their boats as the Inupiat, hunting whale and seal over hundreds of miles of icy ocean.

And boats just make so much more sense. I got an inkling of this as I stood on an oyster-strewn beach with Brian Kingzett and regarded the precipitous wall of tangled rainforest rising above us. "Now you see why the natives almost never went inland," Kingzett said. "The only way to move through the bush was to get down on your hands and knees and crawl along existing game trails. Well, guess who made those trails? That guy over there." He pointed down the beach to a black bear scowling at us. If I couldn't find a reason to plunge into the bush, I doubt the first visitors could either.

As the archaeologist James Dixon has pointed out, if America's first visitors were coastal dwellers, they would have stuck to what they knew:

> The coastal route provides the environmental avenue essential for the initial human entry to the Americas. The coast formed part of a continuous marine coastal-intertidal ecosystem extending between northeastern Asia and northwestern North America and farther south to the southern hemisphere. It would have facilitated coastal navigation and provided similar subsistence resources in a continuous ecological zone linking Asia and North America . . . Coastal environments provide many ecological advantages for generalized foragers, an economic adaptation best suited for colonizing populations. For example, intertidal resources, such as shellfish, may be harvested by the children and the elderly, and simply eaten raw.

It's about as easy as it gets. If your people have always lived along the shore, eating the abundant clams, oysters, mussels, abalone, kelp, and marine mammals, then that's what you do, too. You know how to make boats and fish hooks. You know where to find tasty sea urchins. In contrast, if presented with a grumpy mammoth, "lunch" might not be the first thought that came to mind. You'd probably have followed rivers inland, switching from shellfish to salmon, but forests would have looked as daunting and impenetrable to you as they did to the first European colonists. Eventually, some risk takers would have decided to see what inland life was like. But that would have come much later.

And in a boat, your whole family can move fast. Instead of dragging Grandma and the toddlers through the bush in pursuit of giant mammals, you just load them and all your gear into a hide boat—the minivan of the Stone Age—and follow what Jon Erlandson, director of the University of Oregon's Museum of Natural and Cultural History, calls the kelp highway: "The fact that productive kelp forests are found adjacent to some of the earliest coastal archaeological sites in the Americas supports the idea that such forests may have facilitated human coastal migrations around the Pacific Rim near the end of the last glacial period. In essence, they may have acted as a sort of kelp highway."

Kelp forests are one of the most productive ecosystems on earth. They create food and shelter for numerous species, from fish and shellfish to crustaceans, seals, and sea otters. Growing in ten or twenty feet of water, they form an edible wall of vegetation that serves as a baffle for waves, creating a lane of relatively gentle water filled with snack food. "I've worked on many early sites near kelp forests from Alaska to California," Erlandson has said, "but I never realized similar habitats were present around much of the Pacific Rim."

After a break in the tropics, the kelp highway picks up again in South America, which helps explain one of the festering points in the side of the Clovis argument. For thirty years, an anthropologist named Tom Dillehay, now at Vanderbilt University, has been excavating an ancient settlement in southern Chile known as Monte Verde. The site contains the remains of a dozen huts located on the bank of a river that ran through a peat bog and emptied into a marine bay about ten miles from the settlement. Dillehay found hides, wooden tent stakes, and stone tools. Initial carbon dating showed the artifacts to be a thousand years older than those found in the Clovis sites—in a place ten thousand miles from Beringia. How on earth had the people made it there so early?

Dillehay's initial announcement was so controversial that his funding was cut off. Eventually he found new support and kept on excavating, releasing a new study in 2008 that ended the argument. Rigorous analysis showed the site to be more than fourteen thousand years old. Its inhabitants were not big-game hunters. They left evidence of shellfish, llamas, vegetables, nuts, and nine species of seaweed. "Finding seaweed wasn't a surprise," Dillehay said, "but finding five new species in the abundance we found them was. There are other coastal resources at the site. The Monte Verdeans were really like beachcombers. The number and frequency of these items suggests very frequent contact with the coast, as if they had a tradition of exploiting coastal resources." I wouldn't be surprised if they were the offshoot of an older village located on that bay—a village whose remains are now two hundred feet underwater.

Even if Monte Verde was the first village in the region, the existence of a coastal settlement in southern Chile a thousand years older than Clovis indicates that the coast was settled first. It was the initial draw. The Monte Verdeans may even be a perfect example of the transitional phase when humans were still attached to the coast but were beginning to experiment with resources like nuts and llama meat. But for them, the sea still came first.

Even the Clovis people might not have been quite the big-game hunters they were thought to be. Surprisingly, of the thousands of Clovis spear points that have been found, only a handful show clear evidence of being used in mammoth or bison hunts. The abundance of evidence at Clovis sites indicates the people hunted small animals and foraged for a variety of plant foods. Clovis societies feasted on mammoth about as often as we dine on prime rib. The reality is that human beings kept hugging the coast, from Beringia sixteen thousand years ago to Chile fourteen thousand years ago, because it provided them with everything they needed.

It also compelled them to keep moving. When you occupy an ecosystem that is thousands of miles long but only a hundred yards wide, your movement is linear. You settle on a stretch of coastline rich in shellfish and seaweed. Maybe you move seasonally to take advantage of a good salmon stream. But first the oysters run out, then the clams. Not a problem, because your sons noticed some rich beds a few miles down the coast when they were hunting seals one day. So you move the campsites to the new beds and settle in for a few more years of fine dining. And when those, too, run out, it's time for the next hop. And so it goes, the temperature steadily improving as your children and grandchildren paddle down the Americas in pursuit of the endless raw bar.

THE FOOD THAT MADE US HUMAN

IF SHELLFISH-RICH ESTUARIES were what brought us to the New World and helped define our relationship to it, the question remains: Where on earth did this love affair begin? As Jonathan Swift observed, "He was a bold man that first eat an oyster."

A few of those bold proto-foodies were hanging out 164,000 years ago in a coastal cave on the tip of South Africa with a bird's-eye view of the roaring surf. There, a group of humans enjoyed a leisurely feast of mussels popped open in the embers of a fire and giant periwinkles and whelks fished from their shells with bladelets—expertly made, razorlike stone chips set into wooden handles, much like X-Acto knives. As the sun set into the Indian Ocean, one of the clan began doodling with red ochre. It was just another day in the life of this group as they survived a cold and arid world by gathering food from the only abundant area they knew—the shore. But it would prove to be a momentous feast in 2007, when a team of paleoanthropologists uncovered the evidence. That's because, according to the experts, these early humans shouldn't have been eating shellfish or making art for another forty thousand years. And they shouldn't have been using bladelets for another one hundred thousand years.

Apparently this clan didn't get the memo. And by engaging in what Curtis Marean, the team's lead researcher, calls "key elements of modern behavior"—creativity, symbolic thinking, and sophisticated use of technology—they gave us tremendous insight into our own origins. According to Marean, "We believe that on the far southern shore of Africa there was a small population of modern humans who struggled through this glacial period using shellfish and advanced technologies, and symbolism was important to their social relations. It is possible that this population could be the progenitor population for all modern humans."

We've long known that modern humans, with modern brains, evolved around two hundred thousand years ago, when our lineage experienced a sudden explosion in brain capacity. What we don't know is why. Evolution doesn't happen on a whim; something in the environment needs to change to make the adaptation advantageous.

Stephen Cunnane, a metabolic physiologist at Quebec's University of Sherbrooke who specializes in brain development, has a novel answer to this quandary. Our complex brains require tremendous amounts of energy and very particular nutrients, especially docosahexaenoic acid (DHA), the most important of the omega-3 fatty acids. DHA, which is abundant only in fish and shellfish, is behind fish's "brain food" reputation. It is used to build the cell membranes in the brain and to optimize the connections between neurons. It determines how fast our microprocessors can run. Reduce DHA, says Norman Salem, a neurobiologist with the National Institutes of Health, and "from neuron to neuron, or from the retina to the brain, those signals will still go, but they may be slower and not as intense."

This is still a concern. A 2007 *Lancet* study of nearly twelve thousand women in England found that those who ate fewer than three servings of fish per week while pregnant had children with inferior depth perception, fine-motor coordination, learning abilities, verbal acuity, and social skills, and higher rates of depression. Other studies have found a strong association between postpartum depression and reduced fish consumption—which makes sense, since mothers transfer so much of their DHA to their infants. And the latest supplement for children suffering from autism, dyslexia, depression, and especially attention deficit disorder is an oldie but a goody: fish oil.

"Grandma was right," Dr. Edward Hallowell, founder of the Hallowell Center for Cognitive and Emotional Health, said in the *New York Times*. "Cod liver oil is good for you."

The plants and animals of the savannas and forests, on the other hand, contain virtually no DHA. We can generate a little DHA in our bodies using other omega-3s found in terrestrial foods, but not enough for optimal brain function.

There's wide agreement that switching from a leafy to a fleshy diet powered a lot of the changes we see in hominids leading up to humans. Two million years ago, our ancestors already had a smaller jaw and teeth more adapted to meat than to intense mastication of fibrous plant foods. But, in addition to the DHA problem, on the savannas our ancestors also faced a chicken-or-the-egg dilemma: In order to get the big brain, they needed to eat the meat, but in order to catch the meat, they needed the big brain to make the tools. Today's African hunter-gatherers, with modern tools and full-size brains, still have surprisingly low success rates during hunts. Even my Vermont friends, with rifles and high-powered scopes, have trouble bagging a deer. It's hard to imagine our small-brained forerunners outcompeting the other predators and scavengers of the Serengeti on a regular basis.

For those living on the shore, however, it would have been different. Indeed, since we know that, in groups from grizzly bears to traditional societies, females with kids in tow are the usual clam diggers, then males may well have been off chasing bigger sport while the females quietly gathered shellfish, cracking them open and sliding the soft meat into their toddlers' mouths. They may even have fed the men who came home empty-handed.

What would have compelled us to sample such a radically different type of food in the first place? Was he a bold man that first ate an oyster, or a desperate one? About 195,000 years ago, a lot of our inland food supply dried up—literally. An ice age arrived, forming glaciers across the northern hemisphere and turning much of Africa into a desert. According to Curtis Marean, "The paleoenvironmental data indicate there are only five or six places in all of Africa where humans could have survived these harsh conditions." The drought proved to be a blessing in disguise, because it compelled us to follow some dying river down to a bay, where we encountered something brand new that would change us forever: the sea. We probably wandered stretches of sand beaches, gazing at the waves and feeling the first stirrings of wanderlust, but the more meaningful places for us were the estuaries, thick with oysters and crabs and mussels.

We'd hit the mother lode. We exchanged fruits for fruits of the sea. We developed a taste for seawatery saltiness. In addition to DHA, our new coastal foods were the only ones on earth rich in all the nutrients required for building and maintaining complex brains—iron, copper, zinc, selenium, and especially iodine. As Stephen Cunnane puts it, "Food is commonly more abundant on shorelines than anywhere else . . . Brain expansion on the human scale necessitated sustained access to shellfish and other shore-based foods that are naturally richer in iodine than inland plants and animals."

This "shore-based theory" also explains an evolutionary mystery: Why are our babies so darn fat? No other terrestrial species has chubby infants. Chimp newborns, for instance, are virtually fat-free. They also can fend for themselves in short order, unlike our kids, helpless at four and still struggling to make their own breakfast at eight. How did such a fat, immobile, extended infancy ever become advantageous to survival?

The answer, again, is DHA and shorelines. Baby fat is incredibly rich in DHA and other brain compounds. It is, basically, a three-month starter pack of raw material for the brain—a buffer; the rest has to come from a steady supply in the diet. Any gap in the supply of DHA or iodine during early childhood that is too large to be bridged by baby fat means that full mental abilities won't be achieved.

Clearly, as Cunnane explains in his book *Survival of the Fattest*, we evolved in a world where acquiring those fantastic mental attributes was worth the huge investment of time and resources in slow-maturing, brainy kids. Having a big and creative brain was valuable. And, since any significant disruption in the supply of DHA, iodine, iron, or the other key brain nutrients during prenatal or postnatal development impairs mental abilities, the supply of these nutrients must have been secure. It was also a world where babies' extended helplessness was not a problem—predation must have been light, and long-distance roaming for food wasn't necessary, or was accomplished in boats.

We took to the shore like old salts. Just as improved diets have made recent generations of Westerners taller, so our ancient ancestors, wading through the shellfish beds and mangrove estuaries of the littoral realm, became the smartest dudes in the room. We had time to tinker. We invented better blades, hooks, spears, and boats, not to mention a complex social life. And we became masters at play, the parent of innovation.

It doesn't take a genius to observe that children at play are powerhouses of creativity. They invent new games and rules to accompany them, then they teach those games to the younger children. The science essayist Lewis Thomas has speculated that one of their free-play inventions was language itself:

> I suggest that it began in the children, and it probably began when the earliest settlements, or the earliest nomadic tribes, reached a sufficient density of population so that there were plenty of very young children in close contact with each other, a critical mass of children, playing together all day long. They would already have learned the names of things and people from their elders, and all that remained for them to do was to string the words together so that they made sense. For this, they used the language centers in their brains, assembling grammar and constructing syntax . . . In that moment, human culture was away and running.

Thomas, like Cunnane, recognizes that it is the luxury of play—a luxury nurtured by a high-quality diet in a safe and stable environment where there was no pressure for quick maturation—that allowed us to become brainy, problem-solving modern humans:

> The long period of childhood is not just a time of fragile immaturity and vulnerability, not just a phase of development to be got through before the real show of humanity emerges onstage. It is the time when the human brain can set to work on language, on taste, on poetry and music, with centers at its disposal that may not be available later on in life. If we did not have childhood, and were able somehow to jump catlike from infancy to adulthood, I doubt very much that we would turn out human.

But we did. And the world had never seen anything like us. As each generation taught their games and discoveries to the next, a world of art, technology, and culture bloomed.

We spread around the southern rim of Africa by 164,000 years ago, probably earlier. By 125,000 years ago we were harvesting oysters from the reefs of the Red Sea. There, in 2000, on a fossilized reef along a classic bay on the coast of Eritrea, archaeologists found stone hand axes and flaked obsidian blades among the remains of an oyster feast, along with the shells of crabs, clams, and scallops. "We would like to call this the first oyster bar," said Robert Walter, the team leader.

You can trace a surprisingly clear line from those early humans in Africa right to America's first beachcombers, and that line hugs the coast. The combined archaeological, genetic, and climatological evidence shows us peopling the coasts of Africa for tens of thousands of years. Then we make the leap into Arabia, crossing the narrow Red Sea perhaps eighty thousand years ago. With sea levels hundreds of feet lower than today's, we could practically have walked from Eritrea to Indonesia. Sumatra, Java, Borneo, and many other current islands were all part of the mainland.

Then, about fifty thousand years ago, things got warm and wet again. Relatively stable sea levels allowed new reefs and estuaries to develop, expanding that incredibly productive coastal habitat, and we filled southeast Asia. In only five thousand years we had spread throughout Indonesia and Australia. The amount of charcoal found in sediment deposits from this time indicates that we were sufficiently populous and advanced to be burning a lot of wood from Australia to China.

By thirty-seven thousand years ago we'd reached Japan and the Siberian coast. Even with the lower sea levels at that time, getting to Australia and Japan would have required crossing as much as sixty miles of ocean. Even Michael Phelps's ancestors weren't making that swim. Yet the fossils are there, leading to an inescapable conclusion, summarized by geologist Kevin Pope and archaeologist John Terrell in a 2008 article on coastal migration data: "While the sea level was much lower than it is today when modern

humans first colonized south and east Asia, the archaeological record confirms that the southern coastal migration
of modern humans involved the use of water craft. The
use of such craft may in part explain the rapid dispersal, as
long voyages may have been a common practice in the
search for optimal coastal environments."

Amazingly, a decent stand-in for those peripatetic
coastal dwellers still exists—and I don't mean Brian Allen,
though I had those thoughts as I watched his dark, shiny,
wet-suited head pop to the surface for a breath every couple of minutes as he dove for our dinner. Today, the Moken people of Thailand and Myanmar's Andaman Sea,
commonly known as the sea gypsies, may well be the closest living approximates to those classic humans of forty
thousand years ago. For thousands of years, the Moken
have lived a nomadic and littoral life, traveling in small,
handmade wooden boats called *kabang*. What few posses-
sions they own travel in the kabang with them. They dive
to harvest oysters, sea cucumbers, and fish, frequently
moving to new areas to avoid overharvesting any one
place. They are extraordinarily amphibious. Moken children learn to dive very early in life. Experiments have
shown that they are uniquely able to constrict their
pupils, giving them twice the underwater vision of us
landlubbers.

The Moken were largely unknown to the outside world
until the tsunami of 2004. Before the giant waves hit, the
Moken fled into the coastal mountains. Not a single one
died in the tsunami. When asked later how they knew the

tsunami was coming, they simply replied, "The fish told us." The story received worldwide attention.

By thirty-two thousand years ago we were massed on the northeastern coast of Asia, skilled in coastal living, mariners of the kelp highway, ready for our invasion of Beringia and North America. And then things got ugly. After fifteen thousand years of relative balm, the climate took a nosedive. The Ice Age came on fast and furious. True, this lowered sea levels and opened up Beringia, but it also presented the humans in the area with a climate harsher than any they'd faced. We seem to have hunkered down and even retreated for a good ten thousand years, slowly adapting to life in Siberia. By the time the glaciers peaked around eighteen thousand years ago and retreated, we were ready for the journey to the New World.

By then, of course, many of us had also moved inland. What a mistake. As we left our seafood diet behind, bad things began to happen. "Suddenly," as Stephen Cunnane puts it, "the four-million-year-old freight train of brain expansion ground to a halt . . . In fact, the freight train has been slowly reversing since then." Starting about thirty thousand years ago, our brains began to shrink at a rate four times faster than the previous expansion. Today our brains average 1,360 grams in weight, a full 130 grams less than our illustrious coastal ancestors, and even 60 grams less than the brains of Neanderthals. We are hurtling back toward chimpdom.

It's no coincidence that coastal civilizations have dominated most of history. Part of the problem for inland dwellers is access to iodine, which is found in abundance only in fish, shellfish, and seaweed. The thyroid's key nutrient, iodine is used to regulate metabolism, including the energy allocations during the building of the body and brain. Thousands of years ago, Greek and Chinese physicians prescribed seaweed for goiters, enlarged thyroid glands caused by iodine deficiency. Extreme iodine deficiency causes cretinism, whose symptoms include mental retardation, short stature, a protruding forehead and brow ridge, and dense bones and muscles—the classic "cave man" features. In Indonesia, iodine deficiency is responsible for 800,000 cretins and 1.5 million mentally retarded children—but none in the fishing villages. Rather than anything as obvious as cretinism, the more insidious effect of iodine deficiency is moderate mental impairment—slowness. In a 2008 *New York Times* op-ed, Nicholas Kristof called iodine "a miracle substance that is cheap and actually makes people smarter." He went on to describe the grave situation caused by iodine-deficient diets: "When a pregnant woman doesn't have enough iodine in her body, her child may suffer irreversible brain damage and could have an I.Q. that is 10 to 15 points lower than it would otherwise be. An educated guess is that iodine deficiency results in a needless loss of more than 1 billion I.Q. points around the world."

This loss would be much worse if most of the world's table salt weren't iodized, a practice implemented less than a century ago. The human body doesn't conserve iodine; no matter how little comes in, the same amount goes out. What this means is that our bodies must have evolved in an environment in which iodine was so plentiful that there was never any point in developing a mechanism to hoard it. That hasn't worked out so well for the developing world, whose access to iodized salt is spotty at best. But those billion IQ points down the drain make you realize how much worse the situation must have been until the introduction of iodized salt. Agriculture may have allowed us to bring more calories out of the land than ever before, to create many more people and populate the prairies, but it came with a terrible tradeoff. Corn, rice, wheat, and the other grains that provide the bulk of our calories come in a nutrient package that is more appropriate for a thick-witted buffalo than a human being.

Much of the damage happens in our earliest years, or even before birth, but it continues throughout life. Diabetes, cardiovascular disease, Alzheimer's disease, even depression are all connected to the modern, "civilized" diet. In fact, new studies show that fish oil—primarily DHA—is effective in treating most of the diseases of modern civilization. It reduces the risk of sudden death by heart attack by 90 percent. It lowers blood pressure and heart rate, prevents stroke and diabetes, and reduces inflammation. It prevents Alzheimer's disease and successfully treats Crohn's disease. It slows the growth of cancers and increases the body's healing abilities. It prevents depression and bipolar disorder. It reduces pathological behavior in children and adults, correlates strongly with lower murder rates, and, in one UK experiment, reduced violence among prisoners by 37 percent.

Does all this mean that DHA is a wonder drug we've

been fortunate enough to stumble upon? That, miraculously, seafood happens to cure all our ills? Of course not. It means that our brains and bodies evolved to make full use of DHA and other coastal nutrients, and that when we're cut off from that supply, diseases develop. Joseph Hibbeln of the National Institutes of Health, not exactly a radical organization, is clear about these implications: "Four to five million years of human evolution occurred in a seafood-rich nutritional environment . . . What happens when the nutritional environment radically changes?" I would say it this way: We can achieve peak performance only when fed the high-test fuel found amid the shellfish beds and fish stocks of the littoral zone. We were made for—and made by—that thin world where land meets sea.

Perhaps this explains the seaside vacation, the genetic longing for a landscape we may never have known personally. We play along the coast with friends, cousins, nieces and nephews, splashing in the waves and collecting seashells, making fires on the beach, not understanding why it feels so good. Not realizing that we have returned to the place where being human began.

The shore-based theory of human origins is controversial. Some researchers believe that, given an ideal diet of the right meats and plants, early hunter-gatherers could have synthesized an adequate supply of DHA from land-based omega-3 fatty acids. We don't know for sure. What we do know is that, just as our species was getting its wobbly sea legs under it, shellfish communities helped us navigate some dire straits. Now it's time to return the favor.

MAPS AND MAZES

T HE FOG FOUND us at last. As the softened contours
and ghostly forms along the shores slipped past the
Atrevida, I could feel the presence of that fecund new world
that had emerged thousands of years ago. After two days of
surveying the head of Port Eliza Inlet in Club Med–like
conditions, we had one last morning to work before retreating to Gold River and our regular lives. Drippy white
mist covered the inlet. Which was just fine. Sun and warmth
are great, but this was the raincoast, after all.

We decided to use our last hours to document the pocket beaches dotting the dark green flanks of the inlet. We'd been eyeing these each day as we glided in. They were tiny, some no bigger than a good-size lawn, each bisected by the creek responsible for its creation. I thought again of the I Ching hexagrams, of the oysters perched on those little shelves of constant flux, hardness and softness, wet and dry changing with the days and the seasons. The hexagram to capture this place would be *Meng*, Water under Mountain, an image of a stream emerging from the peaks and hesitating on the edge of an abyss. To the ancients, this symbolized youth, embryonic wisdom that would flourish only with tender cultivation. Like so many of the hexagrams, it concludes with simple advice: "Perseverance furthers."

Brian Kingzett dropped a two-person team on each pocket beach. Mike Beck and I hopped off the inflatable and waded onto a beach on the eastern shore of the inlet, the first anyone had checked on that side. It took us all of about three seconds to see that this one was special. The red and black cobble was gilded with a continuous sheen of Olys. It was unlike any Oly bed I'd seen: almost no algae, few clamshells or wood debris, not even many mussels—just solid Olys nestled into the cobble.

Our excitement rising, we almost ran across the beach, staring awestruck at the dazzling productivity beneath our feet. "Look at this!" Mike said. "These oysters are the dominant life form on this beach. They *are* the structure." They were defining how life expressed itself in that place. They were an ecosystem in miniature.

The entire microhabitat owed its existence to the most modest of rivulets wending its way through the beach. In spring, of course, it would have been anything but modest; swollen and turbid, it would have come surging out of the mountains with enough force to scour the beach, and it showed. No fine sediment here, just chunky cobble that had been sandblasted clean and oysters clinging almost everywhere.

As Brian Allen had observed for the beach at the head of the inlet, there was no oldness here. But there was ancientness. Every few years a powerful storm turned the creek into a pressure washer, fanning across the delta and blasting away everything except the most tenacious Olys. And the oysters came right back. When Brian had looked at his water samples under the microscope, he'd seen plenty of Oly larvae in the water column. As soon as that clean, beautiful hard cobble opened up and the remaining oysters spawned, flooding the water with survivor genes, they'd recolonize it. And they'd probably been doing so, living in a state of eternal youth, for thousands of years.

I'd wondered how such a seemingly fragile animal could ever have been robust enough to support a natural community—and eventually a human one—from California to Alaska, but here on this oyster bed that we'd assigned the humble name of Pocket Beach #3, I understood that these oysters were not so fragile. Disturbance? They didn't mind disturbance. For millennia, they'd withstood everything the tumultuous Northwest could throw at them—glaciers, black Pacific storms, sixteen-armed sea stars, hungry First Nations, and rapacious frontiersmen with sacks and barges. It was all, in a sense, variations on the hundred-year storm, something they'd weathered a thousand times. But the incessant and insidious flow from farms and towns, burying their ancestral lands in muck, was new and different, a problem they couldn't solve. And so a few Puget Sound survivors clung to each other, trying to stay above the rising slime, and the rest retreated to sparkling redoubts like Port Eliza Inlet and persevered, waiting for us humans to quite literally clean up our act.

Cormac McCarthy ends *The Road*, his novel of post-apocalyptic America, with a eulogy for brook trout. "On their backs were vermiculate patterns," he writes, "that were maps of the world in its becoming. Maps and mazes. Of a thing which could not be put back. Not be made right again. In the deep glens where they lived all things were older than man and they hummed of mystery." He could as easily be describing the backs of salmon, or of sunlight playing over the living mazes of an oyster bed.

This is what Mike had come looking for. It's why he'd made the effort to carve a week out of one of the most packed and peripatetic schedules I'd ever heard of. Because the Nature Conservancy had recognized that places like this one—places where the living shore was still intact—were maps to the world in its becoming. That they could help us make things right again.

We had just a few short hours to gather data, to learn what made this postage stamp of a beach so vibrant. While Mike snapped photos and measured the bed from end to end, I tossed my quadrat over my shoulder, watched it land, sat cross-legged beside it, and counted oysters. And counted. And counted.

As I worked my way through this unbroken quilt, pulling out oyster after oyster from the quadrat and piling them all neatly beside it, so lost in the details that I forgot where I was, I flashed for a moment to the monumental piles lining the Northwest coast like lighthouses, and the people thousands of years before me who had made them, equally absorbed in their work and unaware of its connections to anything but that moment. They were the landscape, and for a fleeting instant, so was I.

I finished my count. One hundred and forty-eight tiny oysters, making their home on this quarter meter of tideland.

By then, the others had joined us, and Mike posed a question that has yet to be answered. "From a conservation perspective," he asked, "what would you do about something like this? It probably isn't the only beach like it on the coast, but say there's three or four, and maybe another ten like the one at the head of the inlet. And that's it. *In the world.* What would you do?"

The tide was rising; it was time to go. I took my little scale-model midden and returned the oysters to the bare spot, one at a time, repairing the rift. I had no idea if it made any difference, but I did it anyway. Maybe none of it matters. But maybe all of it does.

ACKNOWLEDGMENTS

A big nod of gratitude to my eight companions on the Vancouver Island trip: Brian Allen, Mike Beck, Sarah Davies, Joth Davis, David Hyde, Brian Kingzett, Betsy Peabody, and Stephanie Richards. It was an amazingly collegial and stimulating group; I can't remember a week of my life when I've learned more. I'm in awe of our host, Bob Devault, for his vast knowledge of the raincoast's culture and natural history; his promptings sent me in many fruitful directions.

It was Tim Jones who helped me realize that this story would make "a nice little book." If not for those early conversations with him and Michael Fisher, I might never have started.

While I was writing the book, John Harper, Curtis Marean, Kevin Pope, Gary Paul Nabhan, Mark Gagliano, Mike Beck, and Robert Brumbaugh were extremely generous with their information, and Betsy Peabody, Brian

Allen, and Brian Kingzett made sure I had my facts straight; it's a better book for their input. It's also better for Kathy Belden's edit; working with her is so painless that I almost take it for granted. It's been nice getting a chance to work with Mary Elder Jacobsen, too; her graceful hand has helped this project become what it was meant to be.

RESOURCES

I have great hope for the littoral communities of the world, because more people and organizations are working to restore them than would have been believed just a few years ago. Here are summaries of the work being done by various groups. For more information or to get involved, visit their Web sites.

Puget Sound Restoration Fund

www.restorationfund.org

What *hasn't* the Puget Sound Restoration Fund been doing? When not organizing expeditions to Nootka Island, Betsy Peabody and the gang have stuck to their mission, staying out of political wrangles and bringing together businesses, tribes, private landowners, and community groups to achieve a heartening number of successful projects throughout Puget Sound, including

- raising abalone to help recover wild populations;
- enhancing twenty-five acres of Oly habitat;
- planting more than ten million Oly seed at promising locations;
- revegetating many acres of riverbanks throughout the watershed;
- restoring water quality in 575 acres of Drayton Harbor so shellfish could again be farmed and harvested;
- launching sixty shellfish gardens and three community shellfish farms to restore clean water and connect people to healthy marine waters; and
- planting hundreds of thousands of oysters to alleviate nutrient loads.

Most intriguing of all, Betsy Peabody and Joth Davis are planning a Native Shellfish Recovery Center on Puget Sound that will produce native species for ecosystem restoration, research, and aquaculture; showcase the native foods that Puget Sound can produce; and help revive a culture that celebrates sustainable resource use.

Deep Bay Field Station

www.mala.ca/csr/facilities/fieldsites.asp

Vancouver Island University's Centre for Shellfish Research is building the unique Deep Bay Field Station, to be managed by Brian Kingzett, which will be the first facility I know of to combine research in shellfish aquaculture and marine ecology with a culinary program and an outreach program geared toward schools and tourists. What I like about the Deep Bay Field Station is that it will connect all the pieces of the puzzle. The facility will be housed in a Leadership in Energy and Environmental Design–certified building that looks out on one of the world's great shellfish-growing bays, showing visitors where their shellfish come from and helping them understand that shellfish farming works only in a healthy ecosystem. And by including a culinary program, it will put everything in place to grow the sustainable industry that can keep that ecosystem clean and productive. In so doing, it will become a twenty-first-century model of the type of all-encompassing shellfish culture that has thrived along the Pacific Northwest raincoast for ten thousand years, and I look forward to seeing what it can accomplish.

The Nature Conservancy's Shellfish Restoration Network

www.nature.org/initiatives/marine/strategies/shellfish.html

The Shellfish Restoration Network, established by the Nature Conservancy, is the point group when it comes to shellfish restoration; the restoration program director is Rob Brumbaugh (rbrumbaugh@tnc.org, 401-874-6870).

The Nature Conservancy has innumerable projects in the works, and is a partner in the following projects, among others:

Gulf Coast, Texas and Louisiana

If you want to get excited about what a well-planned partnership between oysters and human beings can do, watch ReefBLK's slideshow at www.reefblk.com. A system designed by Mark Gagliano, an oyster scientist in Texas, ReefBLK involves a triangular metal framework, hollow in the middle, and about six feet on each side and four feet high. The sides are encased in plastic mesh so they can be filled with clean oyster shell. The structures are set in a row along a shoreline so that they are just underwater. Larvae attach to the shell, and within a year a living reef has formed.

Working at the Nature Conservancy's Mad Island Marsh Preserve in Texas, Gagliano installed ReefBLK units along a thousand-foot stretch of the intercoastal waterway that had been badly eroded by wave surges from barge traffic. Watching the progress of the project is like playing a movie of the degradation of the South's wetlands in reverse. The wall of units was placed a good hundred feet in front of the shoreline—a two-foot mud cliff constantly falling into the water. Instantly, the shoreline stopped eroding as the ReefBLK units absorbed the wave energy. Sediment began to settle in the calm "pool" on the inside of the wall. "We actually captured land," said Gagliano. Ten months later, the land was considerably rebuilt and vegetation was creeping back. The ReefBLK units had transformed into a living reef of yearling oysters that could stand up to storm surges and barge traffic. And a whole new ecosystem was forming around them. "We were dumbfounded by the amount of grazing by drum and sheepshead," Gagliano said. The fish crunched up small oysters, and the crushed shell bits eventually washed ashore and became a layer of protective "mulch" on top of the newly formed beach. Crabs and shrimp filled the reef, and soon egrets were balancing on top of the ReefBLK units as they fished.

ReefBLK systems are now being implemented throughout the Southeast and even as far north as Chesapeake Bay and Long Island Sound.

Narragansett Bay, Rhode Island

In November 2008, the first batch of oysters of a new three-year program funded by the U.S. Department of Agriculture were planted in Narragansett Bay, once the home of an oyster industry that sent thousands of bushels to Hartford, Connecticut, and New York. The goal is to restore sixteen acres of reefs in Narragansett Bay and the salt ponds of Rhode Island's southern coast. What's remarkable about this program is that it's entirely industry-based and takes advantage of more than a century of oyster-growing know-how. Eight Rhode Island shellfish farmers grow the oyster seed until it is large enough to withstand predators, then deploy it on the reef sites. A total of twelve million oysters will be deployed. From there, it's up to them.

Indian River Lagoon, Florida

Florida's Indian River Lagoon, snugged inside Canaveral National Seashore, is the most diverse estuary in North America. More than four thousand species, including fifty endangered ones, call it home. It has a special place in my heart because it's where I first encountered oysters as a kid. On one shore of the lagoon is a hill covered in laurel and live oak trees. It's an oyster midden, left by the Timucuan Indians a thousand years ago. My family still lives nearby, and every year I visit and take my son to explore the lagoon. The oysters were initially done in by overharvesting, and they haven't been able to recover because, without established reefs in place, new oysters get washed ashore by boat wakes. That's changing, thanks to the "oyster mat," a square, mesh, low-rise variation on ReefBLK devised by Linda Walter, a scientist at the University of Central Florida. The Nature Conservancy has organized thousands of volunteers in Central Florida—from schoolchildren to cruise ship passengers—to tie oyster shells to the mats, which are then attached to each other and to the bottom of the lagoon. From the air, it looks like a giant welcome mat. The shells are held in place, as are the spat that attach to them. In a year, a living oyster reef is born. Already 8,200 mats have been placed in multiple locations, forming twenty acres of

Making oyster mats at Florida's Marine Discovery Center.

reef. Juvenile oysters have recruited on all of them, and sea grasses have filled in the sheltered areas between the reefs and the shoreline mangroves. New Smyrna Beach's Marine Discovery Center (www.marinediscoverycenter .org) is a great place to visit to see the restoration efforts in action.

Great South Bay, New York

Long Island's Great South Bay was the original home of the Blue Point oyster and has always been a fabled shellfish estuary. Like the Chesapeake in miniature, it is just a few feet deep and well protected by a barrier island (Fire Island, in this case). Oysters were eliminated from Great South Bay long ago (though Chris Quartuccio of Blue Water Shellfish has recently started growing them again), but its clam population stayed strong through the 1970s, when half the nation's clams were produced there and it was known as the "clam factory." But, just like the Chesapeake, the unholy trinity of nutrient pollution, overharvesting, and habitat destruction reduced the shellfish population to less than 1 percent of its historic norms.

Water quality in the Great South Bay has recently improved, thanks to efforts to control nutrient loading and to restore eelgrass habitat, and in 2006 the Nature Conservancy planted 3' million baby clams in protected areas of bottomland. A 2008 survey revealed 250 million young clams, so something is going very right, and the bay may once again be on the road to filling Manhattan's bowls with local clam chowder.

Chesapeake Bay, Maryland and Virginia

The latest "State of the Bay" reports from the Chesapeake Bay Foundation are as dire as any in the history of the organization. While little has improved on the Chesapeake, I'm hopeful that a nadir has been reached. That nadir was the proposal by the Maryland Watermen's Association, as well as some other groups that should have known better, to introduce an exotic oyster from China, called the Suminoe, to the Chesapeake. Some evidence suggested the Suminoe was more resistant to Dermo, the disease that has devastated the remaining Chesapeake oysters in recent years, so the attitude seemed to be, *Don't bother solving the imbalances that contributed to the diseases in the first place; don't worry about what other impacts an introduced Asian species might have; just bring anything in so that we can keep the dredges running.*

Fortunately the proposal automatically triggered the generation of an environmental-impact statement (EIS), and not long after we returned from our BC trip in 2008, the long-awaited report was released. Years in the making, it weighed in at more than one thousand pages and cost seventeen million dollars. Yet despite the oversized nature, it was surprisingly sensible. Yes, the report found, the Suminoe oyster was resistant to Dermo and grew faster than the native oyster. But it also had a weaker shell, making it easy prey for crabs and other predators, and didn't thrive as well in low-oxygen conditions or intertidal areas. And since it wasn't as tasty or attractive as the native oyster, its culinary appeal was limited. Balancing these factors against the unknown dangers of introducing this Chinese exotic to the Chesapeake, the report made it clear that there was no compelling reason to take such a risk. Michael Lipford, the Virginia state director for the Nature Conservancy, summed up the viewpoint: "With the right investments and management decisions by the public and private sectors, including our organization, we can have native oyster populations that provide significant ecological and economic benefits—all without the risk of unintended consequences."

The EIS also made clear that restoration wouldn't come cheap. It pegged the cost at seven hundred million dollars over ten years. But it also indicated that given the current conditions and scope of the problem, returning to even 1970 numbers was little more than a pie-in-the-sky dream. Aquaculture, on the other hand, "looks most promising." It can create a sizable industry on the Chesapeake, offer excellent filtration services and perhaps some temporary habitat, and take the pressure off wild stocks.

Though the EIS offered several possible alternatives for how to proceed, all included a moratorium on wild harvests. The moratorium would include a program to put displaced watermen to work heading up the on-water restoration work. You'd think the watermen would be thrilled—guaranteed jobs that kept them on the water helping to save the bay, instead of a few last meager years helping to destroy it—but they were as resistant as ever.

Yet despite the watermen's objections, something of a consensus seems to have been reached. Stop the wild harvest, go with the native oyster for restoration purposes (they don't call it *Crassostrea virginica* for nothing), start in the rivers and other tributaries that are less exposed to some of the environmental pressures, and give the new oysters plenty of structure to protect them. At long last some modest successes are under way, thanks in part to a disease-resistant strain of native oyster developed at the Virginia Institute of Marine Science.

Still, no matter how much energy and creativity is poured into oyster restoration, the Chesapeake won't turn around so long as the muck continues to flow in. The Chesapeake Bay Foundation estimates that 80 percent of the nutrient problem could be fixed by focusing on improvements to sewage treatment plants and reduction of agricultural runoff, at a cost of six billion dollars. That's no small sum, but as federal bailouts go, it looks like a real bargain.

Wellfleet Bay, Massachusetts

The Wellfleet oyster is famous, but the last native Wellfleet was eaten in 1775. After that, oysters had to be imported from Chesapeake Bay to stock the beds. Today most Wellfleets are farmed. But the wild Wellfleet may soon rebound, thanks to a new reef begun in 2008 by the Massachusetts Audubon society (www.massaudubon.org). Volunteers have restored two acres of reef using a mix of cultch, reef balls (concrete cousins to the ReefBLK system), and mats (the Florida approach) to learn what works best in Wellfleet Harbor.

NATIONAL OCEANIC AND ATMOSPHERIC ADMINISTRATION

habitat.noaa.gov/restoration

NOAA is the godfather of coastal restoration efforts. It has funded at least seventy-five oyster restoration projects in fifteen states, and its Restoration Portal Web site is the best place to start learning about the history, science, and current state of oyster restoration.

Oyster Gardener Programs

One of the nicest trends on both coasts of the United States is the rise of oyster gardener programs, in which individuals or organizations with waterfront property volunteer to raise baby oysters in protected bags and cages until they are large enough for conservation organizations to plant them in the estuaries. The popular programs give people a hands-on connection to their home estuaries and a palpable sense of the difference they can make. Some of the organizations with oyster gardener programs are the following:

Chesapeake Bay Foundation (www.cbf.org)
NY/NJ Baykeeper (www.nynjbaykeeper.org)
Puget Sound Restoration Fund (www.restorationfund.org)
Maine Sea Grant (www.seagrant.umaine.edu)
Delaware Center for the Inland Bays (www.inlandbays.org)
Shellfish Gardeners of North Carolina (www.carteret.edu/
    aqu/cogp)
South Carolina Oyster Gardeners (http://scoystergardener.
    blogspot.com)
Rhode Island Oyster Gardening for Restoration and
    Enhancement (www.rwu.edu)
Mobile Bay National Estuary (www.mobilebaynep.com)

RICHARDSON BAY AUDUBON

www.tiburonaudubon.org

News of the San Francisco Oly's death, it turns out, was slightly exaggerated. In 1999, people began spotting tiny oysters along the shoreline of Richardson Bay, a nine-hundred-acre preserve in the northern reaches of San Francisco Bay. Everyone assumed that the bay's severe pollution had wiped out the oysters long ago, but, as we all are learning, the Oly is a survivor. Now Audubon California, which manages the Richardson Bay sanctuary, is spearheading a joint effort by NOAA, the Smithsonian Institute, Save the Bay, and other organizations to revive the oyster and the eelgrass habitat that always seems to accompany it.

COMCA'AC NATIVE AQUACULTURE

http://comcaacnativeaquaculture.blogspot.com

One of the most exciting oyster-recovery projects is under way in Mexico, on the Sonoran coast of the Gulf of California (Steinbeck's Sea of Cortez), where the Seri Indians, or Comca'ac, are cultivating the native Cortez oyster (*Crassostrea corteziensis*). The Seri, an indigenous group that has lived along the coast for as long as anyone can remember, are the last hunter-gatherers of the Pacific shore, eating wild fish, shellfish, and native plants that thrive in the mangrove estuaries of the coast. In this way, they are some of the closest living models of those first humans who lived along the African coast. They have managed to fight off developers wishing to exploit their tropical coastline, but ultimately the temptation of the developers' cash can be defeated only by developing a sustainable way of making a living from their lands and waters. So the Seri have begun an indigenous aquaculture project, cultivating the Cortez oyster in a tribally controlled mangrove estuary using sustainable methods. The first crop of oysters was harvested in fall 2008. In 2009 they became available in Sonoran beach towns, and Steinbeck's ghost is undoubtedly happily hunkered down right now in the darkest corner of the grimiest bar on the coast with a warm cerveza and a plate of Cortezes. By 2010 they should begin appearing in select U.S. restaurants.

Alberto Mellado, tribal aquaculturalist for the Seri, with Cortez oysters.
Photograph by Gary Paul Nabhan.

SOURCES

Associated Press. "30,000 Atlantic Salmon Escape from a BC Fish Farm." *Seattle Post-Intelligencer*, July 4, 2008.

Aubrey, Allison. "Getting Brain Food Straight from the Source." NPR.org, November 1, 2007.

Barry, Cynthia. "A Homecoming for Oysters." *Save the Bay*, Fall 2008.

BC Pacific Salmon Forum. *Final Report and Recommendations to the Government of British Columbia.* www.pacificsalmonforum. ca, January 2009.

Blankenship, Karl. "EIS Predicts Long Recovery for Oysters in the Bay; Is Optimistic for Aquaculture." *Bay Journal*, November 2008.

Brumbaugh, Robert D., and Caitlyn Toropova. "Economic Valuation of Ecosystem Services: A New Impetus for Shellfish Restoration." *Basins and Coasts*, May 2008.

Cunnane, Stephen. *Survival of the Fattest: The Key to Human Brain Nutrition.* Hackensack, N.J.: World Scientific, 2005.

Denny, Carol. "Prophetic Words." *Save the Bay*, Fall 2008.

Dillehay, Tom, et al. "Monte Verde: Seaweed, Food, Medicine, and the Peopling of South America." *Science,* May 9, 2008.

Dixon, E. James. *Bones, Boats, and Bison: Archeology and the First Colonization of Western North America.* Albuquerque: University of New Mexico Press, 1999.

Fahrenthold, David A. "Broken Promises on the Bay." *Washington Post*, December 27, 2008.

Fleeger, John W. "The Potential to Mass-Culture Harpacticoid Copepods for Use as Food for Larval Fish." In *Copepods in Aquaculture*, edited by Cheng-Sheng Lee, Patricia O'Bryen, and Nancy H. Marcus. Hoboken, N.J.: Wiley-Blackwell, 2005.

Gordon, David G., Nancy E. Blanton, and Terry Y. Nosho. *Heaven on the Half Shell: The Story of the Northwest's Love Affair with the Oyster.* Seattle: University of Washington, 2001.

Greer, Jack. "Shadow on the Chesapeake." *Chesapeake Quarterly*, September 2008.

Grescoe, Taras. *Bottomfeeder: How to Eat Ethically in a World of Vanishing Seafood.* New York: Bloomsbury USA, 2008.

Halsey, Ashley. "EPA Called 'A Negative Factor' in Bay Cleanup." *Washington Post*, December 30, 2008.

Harper, John, et al. *Broughton Archipelago Clam Terrace Survey.* Sidney, B.C.: Coastal and Ocean Resources Inc., 1995.

Harrison, Marion. "Meet the Otters." www.canadiangeographic.ca, summer 2006.

Hebda, Richard, et al. *An Ice Age Refugium on Vancouver Island.* Occasional Paper No. 5, B.C. Ministry of Environment, Lands and Parks, Victoria, B.C., 1997.

Hetherington, Renée, et al. "Quest for the Lost Land." *Geotimes,* February 2004.

Hibbeln, Joseph. "Omega-3 Fatty Acids: Depression and Addiction." Food for the Brain Conference, London, UK, October 12, 2008.

Hibbeln, Joseph, et al. "Maternal Seafood Consumption in Pregnancy and Neurodevelopmental Outcome in Childhood (ALSPAC Study): An Observational Cohort Study." *Lancet*, February 17, 2007.

House, Freeman. *Totem Salmon: Life Lessons from Another Species.* Boston: Beacon, 1999.

Jackson, Jeremy B. C. "Ecological Extinction and Evolution in the Brave New Ocean." *Proceedings of the National Academy of Sciences*, August 11, 2008.

Jacobsen, Rowan. *A Geography of Oysters: The Connoisseur's Guide to Oyster Eating in North America.* New York: Bloomsbury USA, 2007.

Koppel, Tom. *Lost World: Rewriting Prehistory—How New Science Is Tracing America's Ice Age Mariners.* New York: Atria Books, 2003.

Kristof, Nicholas D. "Raising the World's I.Q." *New York Times*, December 4, 2008.

Little, Jane Braxton. "Bay Watch." *Audubon*, November–December 2008.

London, Jack. *Tales of the Fish Patrol.* Oakland, Calif.: Regent Press, 1914.

Mann, Charles C. *1491: New Revelations of the Americas Before Columbus.* New York: Knopf, 2005.

Manning, Richard. *Against the Grain: How Agriculture Has Hijacked Civilization.* New York: North Point Press, 2004.

Marean, Curtis, et al. "Early Human Use of Marine Resources and Pigment in South Africa During the Middle Pleistocene." *Nature,* October 18, 2007.

McCarthy, Cormac. *The Road.* New York: Knopf, 2006.

McCulloch, Sandra. "Clam Gardens Offer Fresh Aboriginal Insights." *Victoria Times Colonist.* August 28, 2005.

Montgomery, David R. *King of Fish: The Thousand-Year Run of Salmon.* Cambridge, Mass.: Westview, 2003.

"New Evidence About Earliest Americans Supports Coastal Migration Theory." Vanderbilt University press release, May 6, 2008.

Nicholson, George. *Vancouver Island's West Coast, 1762–1962.* Vancouver, B.C.: George Nicholson's Books, 1965.

Peter-Contesse, Tristan, and Betsy Peabody. *Reestablishing Olympia Oyster Populations in Puget Sound, Washington.* Seattle: Washington Sea Grant, 2005.

Pope, Kevin O., and John E. Terrell. "Environmental Setting of Human Migrations in the Circum-Pacific Region." *Journal of Biogeography*, January 2008.

Pope, Kevin O., et al. "Origin and Environmental Setting of Ancient Agriculture in the Lowlands of Mesoamerica." *Science*, May 18, 2001.

Rabin, Roni Caryn. "Feeling Good About Fish Oil." *New York Times*, September 15, 2008.

"Researchers Find Earliest Evidence for Modern Human Behavior in South Africa." Arizona State University press release, October 17, 2007.

Steinbeck, John. *The Log from the Sea of Cortez.* New York: Penguin Modern Classics, 2001.

Thomas, Lewis. *The Fragile Species.* New York: Charles Scribner's Sons, 1992.

United States Army Corps of Engineers. *Draft Programmatic Environmental Impact Statement for Oyster Restoration in Chesapeake Bay Including the Use of a Native and/or Nonnative Oyster.* www.nao.usace.army.mil/oystereis/eis/homepage.asp, 2008.

University of Oregon. "'Kelp Highway' May Have Helped Peopling of the Americas." Press release, February 21, 2006.

Walter, Robert, et al. "Early Human Occupation of the Red Sea Coast of Eritrea During the Last Interglacial." *Nature*, May 4, 2000.

Williams, John Page. *Chesapeake: Exploring the Water Trail of Captain John Smith*. Washington, D.C.: National Geographic, 2006.

Williams, Judith. *Clam Gardens: Aboriginal Mariculture on Canada's West Coast*. Vancouver, B.C.: New Star Books, 2006.

Winthrop, Theodore. *The Canoe and the Saddle*. Lincoln, Neb.: Bison Books, 2006.

INDEX

INDEX

A NOTE ON THE AUTHOR

ROWAN JACOBSEN is the James Beard Award–winning author of *A Geography of Oysters* and *Fruitless Fall*. His writings on food, the environment, and their interconnected nature have appeared in the *New York Times*, *Wild Earth*, *Harper's*, *Eating Well*, and *Newsweek*. He lives in rural Vermont with his wife and son